Bruce R. Fretz
David H. Mills

Licensing and Certification of Psychologists and Counselors

*A Guide to
Current Policies, Procedures,
and Legislation*

 Jossey-Bass Publishers
San Francisco • Washington • London • 1980

LICENSING AND CERTIFICATION OF PSYCHOLOGISTS AND COUNSELORS
A Guide to Current Policies, Procedures, and Legislation
by Bruce R. Fretz and David H. Mills

Copyright © 1980 by: Jossey-Bass Inc., Publishers
433 California Street
San Francisco, California 94104
&
Jossey-Bass Limited
28 Banner Street
London EC1Y 8QE

Library of Congress Cataloging in Publication Data

Fretz, Bruce R   1939-
    Licensing and certification of psychologists and
counselors.

    Bibliography: p. 181
    Includes index.
    1. Psychologists—Certification. 2. Psycholo-
gists—Licenses. 3. Counselors—Certification.
4. Counselors—Licenses. I. Mills, David H.,
joint author. I. Title.
BF80.8.F73   351.82'43   80-8011
ISBN 0-87589-470-4

Manufactured in the United States of America

JACKET DESIGN BY WILLI BAUM

FIRST EDITION

Code 8032

The Jossey-Bass
Social and Behavioral
Science Series

Preface

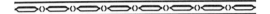

In the past few years, licensing and certification in counseling and psychology have become provocative and controversial topics. At professional conventions, sessions on these topics attract standing-room-only audiences. Leaders and other knowledgeable persons in the counseling and psychology professions receive numerous requests for information and assistance in dealing with state licensing boards, accrediting agencies, boards and commissions, legislators, and attorneys. This book provides the first comprehensive overview of current information on and issues in licensing, certification, and other forms of credentialing for persons trained in counseling programs and psychology programs at the doctoral and master's degree levels.

In our professional roles with licensing and accrediting agencies, boards, and commissions, we have found that most professionals in psychology and counseling are hardly aware of the diversity and magnitude of difficulties encountered by both applicants and reviewers. Consequently, every new batch of psychologists and counselors is unprepared to cope with the problems; the search for information and assistance is usually a painfully lonely and frustrating experience. We hope that the heretofore scattered and often not readily available information in this book can help present and new professionals deal with credentialing problems.

The nine chapters that follow provide information for (1) counselors and psychologists who need to understand and appreciate the origins of current problems in credentialing faced by both neophytes and established colleagues who make professional changes; (2) present and aspiring students in psychology and counseling who should carefully review their current training in light of the requirements for the diverse forms of credentialing; and (3) consumers of psychological and counseling services, many of whom are probably more baffled than professionals by the plethora of credentials and what they represent. Such consumers want to know what the differences are among certified mental health counselors, licensed psychologists, licensed marriage and family therapists, and certified rehabilitation counselors.

Colleagues and students who often cited the dearth of literature on licensing and credentialing issues provided the initial encouragement for this book. Once we began to gather information, many additional colleagues assisted us by sending materials and describing their own troublesome, as well as satisfactory, credentialing experiences. Special thanks for such descriptions are extended to Robert P. Anderson, James W. Lichtenberg, Jon W. McIntire, Samuel H. Osipow, Theodore Packard, Carl D. Swanson, and J. Melvin Witmer. We also appreciate the permission granted by the Council of State Governments to reproduce their listing of legislators' questions. Josephine Shaffer came early and stayed late on more days than she would like to remember to type and retype the many drafts of this manuscript. We are indebted to her for her commitment to the timely completion of this book.

College Park, Maryland   Bruce R. Fretz
July 1980   David H. Mills

Contents

⊂○○⊂○○⊂○○⊂○○⊂○○⊂○○⊂○○⊂

9.   Prospects for Licensing and Certification
     in the 1980s   173

     Appendix   179

     References   181

     Index   190

The Authors

Bruce R. Fretz is professor of psychology and director of the Counseling Psychology Program at the University of Maryland. Fretz received his bachelor's degree (1961) in psychology from Gettysburg College and his master's (1963) and doctor's (1965) degrees in psychology from Ohio State University.

In 1978, Fretz was elected to the Education and Training Board of the American Psychological Association (APA) and serves as board liaison to the APA Committee on Accreditation. In 1979, he was elected to the Board of Examiners for Psychologists in Maryland. Fretz was an active participant in the 1973 Vail Training conference on patterns of professional training in psychology and the 1976 and 1977 APA education and credentialing conferences. In 1976, he was elected a fellow of the APA; he holds the diplomate in counseling psychology. He has written over forty articles published primarily in counseling and psychological journals. The most recent books by Fretz are *The Present and Future of Counseling Psychology* (co-edited with J. Whiteley, 1980) and *Preparing for Graduate Study in Psychology* (with D. Stang, 1980).

David H. Mills is professor of psychology and assistant director of the Counseling Center at the University of Maryland. Mills received his bachelor's degree in economics (1955) and his master's in psychology (1957) from Iowa State University. He earned his doctoral degree in psychology (1964) at Michigan State University and was a postdoctoral fellow in quantitative psychology (1964-65) at the University of Illinois.

Formerly president of the International Association of Counseling Services, Mills is a fellow of the American Psychological Association in which he also serves on the Committee for Professional Standards. A participant in the 1976 and the 1977 APA education and credentialing conferences, he was a member of the APA task force that recently revised accreditation standards. From 1975 to 1979, he worked with the National Register of Health Service Providers in Psychology as a member of the review panel and as a research consultant. Mills is the author of more than fifty articles and book chapters; his current research interest is mental health manpower resources.

Licensing and Certification of Psychologists and Counselors

A Guide to
Current Policies, Procedures,
and Legislation

1

Licenses, Certification, and Credentials

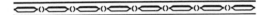

- A licensed psychologist is hired as the director of a university counseling center in a state other than the one in which he is licensed. He moves to the new state, applies for licensing as a psychologist, and is told that he is ineligible for the examination because his training was not in psychology.
- A certified mental health counselor applies for a permit to hang a shingle in his home and is informed, "Your professional occupation is not permitted as a home occupation" (Scelsa, 1979).
- A graduate of a psychology program accredited by the American Psychological Association but not housed in a psychology department is informed that she is ineligible for certification as a psychologist because her training is not in psychology.
- A psychologist trained in physiology offers biofeedback services to the public. He is reported to the state licensing board

for offering mental health services without appropriate training.

· A graduate of a counseling and guidance program that has a
long history of graduating practicing professional psychologists—some of whom have achieved national distinction—is
declared ineligible for the psychology licensing examination
since his degree was not "primarily psychological in nature."

· A student in a clinical psychology program is dropped after
his second year of training because of incompetence; he then
opens up a private practice as a psychotherapist and is careful
not to use the label *psychologist*. The program finds that
neither state law nor the profession's ethics can be invoked to
stop his practice.

· A graduate of a counseling psychology program accredited by
the American Psychological Association applies for a federal
civil service classification and is declared ineligible because
her internship training was "insufficient."

· A graduate of an industrial-organizational program offered by
psychologists in a college of business administration is declared ineligible for licensure as a psychologist since his program was not "primarily psychological in nature."

· A licensed psychologist, whose practica and internship training were supervised by licensed psychologists listed in the National Register of Health Service Providers in Psychology, is
declared ineligible for listing in the register because her degree
is not from an organized psychology program.

· A psychologist lists marriage and family therapy as one of her
services; she is informed by a state licensing board that she
must be certified as a marriage and family therapist in order
to publicize such services.

Introduction

For any psychologist or counselor, these challenges to
one's own professional identity arouse unwanted but, unfortu-
nately, not unwarranted anxiety. In the last few years almost all
of us have received some disquieting information about an
organizational policy or state statute that may affect the nature

of our present work or the career for which we are preparing. What developments and issues have led to this situation? What organizations and statutes significantly affect what psychologists and counselors can do and when and where they can do it? Where can valid information be obtained? Who can provide assistance when regulations or statutes seem unjust? What difficulties encountered by licensing boards and accrediting agencies lead to these problems?

Certainly one major difficulty underlying continuing changes in professional credentialing is the diversity of skills and interests of persons identified as psychologists and counselors. The two major professional organizations in counseling and psychology, the American Personnel and Guidance Association (APGA) and the American Psychological Association (APA), include nearly 100,000 professional persons, thousands of whom engage in similar if not identical functions. Yet each organization also has members whose activities are as contrasting as directing a home for unwed mothers and investigating eye movements.

Given the breadth of the professions, it is not surprising that persons of diverse training and experience have sought credentialing as counselors and psychologists. This situation has created increasing tension in the mainstream of each profession, which has resulted in increasing specification of the training and experience necessary for licensure. Many counselors and psychologists perceive these specifications as a threat to their careers.

In addition to concern about their own careers in psychology or counseling, some professionals as well as consumer advocates are equally concerned about the effects of licensing on auxiliary mental health personnel, such as nonprofessionals, paraprofessionals, ministers, pastoral counselors, and school counselors. Will licensing eventually prohibit the counseling and evaluative services that many of these people provide, usually to people who are not well served by traditional professionals (Lorion, 1979)?

Before continuing, we must issue an important warning. We may be uneasy but quite correct in predicting that the issues discussed here will change little in the near future, although some will become more significant in some states while less so in others. However, we would be both uneasy and incorrect in predicting that the pertinent regulations of the various states and organizations will remain the same in the next few years. Licensing and credentialing in both psychology and counseling are in a state of change. Conflicts in specialties within psychology and counseling, as well as issues outside of the professions such as "sunset legislation," could lead to radical changes in longstanding laws and the implementation of new laws and regulations. Experts expect numerous changes and developments over the next five years and very likely throughout the 1980s. All information in this text was accurate in 1979. Readers wishing to pursue any of the particular types of credentialing described in this book are urged to find out current relevant laws and regulations. Appropriate sources and their addresses are provided in the appendix.

The following chapters discuss various types of licensing and include a brief history of the development of each form of credential as well as a summary of the policies, purposes, and procedures of the accrediting organizations and legislative bodies. Until now most of this information could be obtained only by writing to or being active in each of the accrediting organizations. Thus, it is not surprising that most counselors and psychologists are poorly informed about the many credentialing organizations that affect their careers.

For each type of credentialing the special issues and problems that counselors and psychologists most frequently encounter are described. Examples of attempts to influence policies are included wherever possible. To our knowledge, many of these issues, problems, and recommendations have not been written down, thus creating a kind of folklore about credentialing that only a few people have known—usually those people who work with persons directly involved in credentialing processes.

Chapter Two reviews the history of the regulation of professions as well as the advantages and disadvantages that have been cited most often in arguing for the licensing of counselors and psychologists. From this broad perspective, we hope that the reader will be prepared for Chapters Three, Four, and Five, which address the history and current status of licensing in psychology and counseling. These chapters will make clear that forces both outside of and within our professions determine many career opportunities. Case examples, some of which have reached the courts, help identify the issues that must be addressed.

Counselors and psychologists have been involved in the development and change of state licensing procedures. Legislators themselves are now aware of the advantages and disadvantages of occupational licensing. Chapter Six draws upon the experience of counselors and psychologists who have been involved in state licensing procedures in order to describe the procedures for developing and influencing legislation. The factors reviewed in Chapters Three through Five radically affect licensing laws and require that more members of our professions become involved in the legislative processes if we are to remain viable professions.

Chapters Seven and Eight focus on other types of credentialing, such as the accreditation of training and service programs and nonstatutory, voluntary, and individual credentials. Both chapters identify accrediting organizations and agencies and review their purposes, policies, and procedures. The implications of these types of accreditation for careers are noted, and special issues that counselors and psychologists have encountered with these organizations and agencies are identified. Recommendations are also provided for handling these problems and issues.

The final chapter discusses the prospects for licensing and credentialing in the 1980s. We note the issues that must be addressed and the actions that must be taken by the professions of psychology and counseling if the concerns of both the profession and the public are to be met. An appendix provides the addresses of the many organizations mentioned in the book.

Definitions

The terms *psychologist* and *counselor* provided the authors with considerable difficulty. The term *counselor* can be applied to so many roles that it describes a cast of thousands.

The term *counselor* seems to have been appropriated by anyone who is trying to help anyone with anything. We will use the term to designate a person with a graduate degree in either counseling or counseling and guidance.

The usage of the term *psychologist* has been increasingly prescribed by the APA. In January 1977 it adopted the following position:

> The title "professional psychologist" has been used so widely and by persons with such a wide variety of training and experience that it does not provide the information the public deserves. As a consequence, the APA takes a position and makes it a part of its policy that the use of the title "Professional Psychologist," and its variations such as "Clinical Psychologist," "Counseling Psychologist," "School Psychologist," and "Industrial Psychologist" are reserved for those who have completed a Doctoral Training Program in Psychology in a university, college, or professional school of psychology that is APA or regionally accredited.
>
> The APA further takes the position and makes a part of its policy that only those who have completed a Doctoral Training Program in Professional Psychology in a university, college, or professional school of psychology that is APA or regionally accredited are qualified independently to provide unsupervised direct delivery of professional services including preventive, assessment, and therapeutic services. [Resolution on the Master's Level Issue, 1977].

The authors recognize that over the years many people have been trained in other types of doctoral and master's programs in counselor education and psychology and have considered themselves—indeed, been certified or licensed—as psychologists or counselors. As qualifications for psychologists have become more restrictive, more attention has been given to the licensing and credentialing of counselors as counselors. Therefore, this book includes information regarding master's-level as well as doctoral-level persons trained in the fields of counseling or psychology. However, in the text, the use of the term *psychologist* will be in accord with APA policy and refer only to appropriately trained doctoral-level persons. The term *counselor* will be used as mentioned above for those master's- or doctoral-level persons trained in counselor education or other counselor training programs. For those trained in psychology having master's degrees, the term *master's-level psychologist* will be used.

Other terms must also be defined for this book.

The uses of the terms *licensure, certification, accreditation, designation, registration,* and *listing* have all varied considerably. All of these terms can be subsumed under the term *credentialing*, which the dictionary defines as "giving a title or claim to credit or competence." In contrast to *credentialing*, which is the broadest term, *licensure* is perhaps the most specific. The terms *licensure* and *certification* present yet more difficulties. The APA and the APGA use these terms differently, with the APA's definition being the more narrow. *Licensure* refers to laws that regulate the use of the title and that define those activities that constitute the practice of a particular profession; licensure violations involve greater legal penalties than do violations of other types of credentialing. In the APA perspective, certification regulations are designed only to limit the use of a title, such as psychologist, but not, as in the case of licensure, the scope of practice. Certification can be awarded by fulfilling state requirements or granted by nonstatutory associations or agencies. The APGA position essentially includes statutory certification and licensing according to the APGA definition: *Licensure* is the statutory process by which an agency of government, usually of a state, grants permission to a person meeting predetermined qualifications to engage in a given occupation and/or use a particular title and to perform specified functions. *Certification,* in the APGA position, is the nonstatutory process by which an agency or association grants recognition to an individual for having met certain predetermined professional qualifications. Stated succinctly, certification in the APA position is a "limited license," that is, the protection of title only; APGA uses certification to refer to all types of credentials not derived from statutes; such credentials are described in Chapter Eight. Because of its preciseness, we will adopt the APA position, referring to certification as protection of use of title. The term *credential* is used to refer to the myriad other forms of recognition discussed in Chapter Eight.

Other terms include *accredited program* and *approved program,* both of which describe an educational training or service program in a school or institution that has met certain standards and qualifications as determined by a review of documents and/or by site visits by a team of reviewers. *Designated, registered,* and *listed* are terms that can be used by either institutions or individuals to indicate that they have been publicly identified as meeting certain qualifications and are eligible for formal listing, for example, in the *National Register of Health Service Providers in Psychology* or the *Counselor Education Directory.*

A great deal of confusion and misrepresentation has occurred in the professions because of the inappropriate use of terms. For example, a listing of a program in a directory may be used as evidence of an approved status, or a listing in the APA membership directory as evidence of being a certified psychologist. As we describe each agency or organization in subsequent chapters, we will identify the appropriate uses of and limits to the credentials offered and cite any frequent misapplications of the credentials.

2

Values, Purposes, and Challenges of Licensing

"Raise a flag, and someone will salute." This paraphrase of the old saying is a fitting introduction to a review of the myriad viewpoints in favor of and against professional licensing. Many issues have been raised over the centuries (yes, centuries!) during which professional licensing has been employed; each new profession seems to go through a sequence of an increasingly familiar array of positions, both for and against professional licensing. To provide a broad perspective, the next section reviews the history of the licensing of professions. The major positions in support of and against professional licensing in psychology and counseling are then described, followed by a discussion of regulations that critics of licensing might be likely to accept. Finally, the attitudes of boards of examiners and the current legislative challenges to licensing are surveyed.

9

A Brief History of Credentialing

While trades and professions have been regulated in effect by social class systems since ancient Egypt and Greece (Krause, 1977), the first modern regulation of professions occurred in the thirteenth century, when Frederick II, emperor of the Holy Roman Empire, instituted the first medical practice act (Gross, 1978) to combat the problem of "witches" practicing among the people. Licensing laws prohibited anyone but university-trained physicians from practicing (Ehrenreich and English, 1973). Gross (p. 1010) notes that "though the effectiveness of these laws was limited because of the great need for service and the inability and unwillingness of university trained physicians to serve the masses, it is important to note this early reliance on the authority of the state to legitimize an occupation. This attempt to monopolize medical practice in situations of imbalance between need and available service was unrealistic, given the large number of unlicensed medical advisors, and would eventually lead to a temporary abandonment of licensing in the 19th century in the United States." This imbalance between need and available service continues to be a valid argument against licensing 700 years after the first attempt at licensure!

The decline in licensing in the nineteenth century was short-lived. By the late 1800s, the legal and medical professions promoted systems of regulation that resulted in professional regulation as we know it today (Tabachnik, 1976). "In the 20th century, the trends have been (a) for licensing to include an ever greater number of occupations, (b) for the type of licensing to go from title certification to compulsory licensing of practice and (c) for the raising and tightening of standards—including moving from an apprentice system to one centering on training and educational institutions, lengthening the period of training, and adding internships after training" (Gross, 1978, p. 1011). Mackin (1976) reports that there are now over *2,800* statutes for occupational licensing in the United States.

The history of credentialing and licensing in other professions is a familiar one to psychologists and counselors. As Wellner (1978, p. 74) notes, Flexner, in the 1910 Carnegie Foundation survey of all medical schools in the United States and Canada, "found a tremendous diversity of standards, curricula, and organizations involved in the education of physicians. Flexner was appalled at the number of proprietary schools with few if any of the essential materials and equipment to educate physicians. He was appalled at the lack of academic requirements for entry into medical school and he addressed the problems related to the licensing of the practitioners and the statutorily established criteria and standards for such licensure. Flexner was concerned with the distribution of physicians, the need for an educational system which provides sufficient number of physicians for populations in various segments of the country."

Wellner (1978) provides further details of the Flexner (1910) report, the Reed (1921) report concerning legal education, and the Gies (1926) report on dental education, especially as these latter reports relate to the need for completing accredited training programs as a prerequisite to licensing. Reviewing the accreditation of academic programs and the credentialing of professionals at the present time, Wellner observes the following: (1) In medicine or dentistry the applicant must graduate from an approved or accredited school; (2) in law one need not graduate from an approved school, but a graduate from an approved school is automatically eligible for the bar exam in all states; and (3) in pharmacy some states require graduation from an accredited program in order to be eligible for licensing.

Pros and Cons of Professional Licensing

Most arguments in support of licensing fall under one of the five major premises presented below. For each premise, various rebuttals have appeared in the literature, which are also described. In fact, in the psychological literature, much more appears to have been published *against* licensing than in favor of it; yet licensing legislation has accelerated in the last decade. The bibliography provides references for readers who wish to investigate these issues.

Licensure Protects the Public by Setting Minimum Standards for Service Providers. According to this argument, consumers will be protected from inadequately trained and incompetent practitioners if a profession is properly licensed. In psychology and counseling, as in medicine, dentistry, and pharmacy, this is viewed as an important point, since the damage that can be done by an incompetent practitioner may have lifelong consequences for the user.

In rebutting this premise, opponents usually note that, while the goal may be laudable, licensing does not really protect the public. First, incompetents can merely change their title in order to comply with the law. In a state in which psychologists and counselors are licensed, one can call oneself a "social therapist" or a "personal growth leader." Second, most current licensing laws concern one's training more than one's competence (Hogan, 1979b). Consequently, in the view of many, most licensing laws have in effect legitimized incompetent, if "appropriately" trained, practitioners, while excluding many competent practitioners (Arbuckle, 1977; Moore, 1979; Ivey, 1978). Only recently have states begun to require continuing education in order to renew a license or certificate, while no state presently requires the competence of psychologists to be evaluated periodically. The minimum standard in most psychology licensing laws is the doctoral degree. Thus, thousands of persons who had been recognized as legitimate service providers were excluded from practice when such laws were passed. Hogan (1979b) and Ivey (1978) cite the *lack* of evidence of any correlation between the skills of psychotherapists and their credentials.

People who support licensure usually concede that laws do exclude some "natural helpers" and other "well-trained helpers" who lack doctorates. However, they point out that by setting higher standards, one decreases the number of incompetently trained people, especially since many of the 2,000 annual graduates of master's programs in this country have had little or no practicum training. The rebuttal to this point is that if as much attention were placed on regulating the training and standards for providers with master's degrees as for those with doctorates, the public would be equally protected.

Licensing Protects the Public from Its Own Ignorance. The consumer in need of counseling or psychological services typically does not know how to choose the practitioner or how to judge the nature of the services received. Unlike the effects of a bad appliance repair person, the immediate effects of a bad counselor or psychologist are not so readily apparent.

Hogan (Moore, 1979) argues that licensing actually compounds the public's ignorance by leading the public to believe that it is protected from incompetence. Gross (1978) extends this argument, stating that licensing tends to mystify the therapy experience by reducing the amount of information that is provided to the consumer; for example, licensing laws usually restrict the information that can be advertised. Gross (1977, p. 587), in another article, notes "the most insidious effect of licensing, however, is that it is a major support of a system that creates a dependency on professionals, a dependency that reduces the ability of people to care for themselves. Illich (1976) singles this out as a major component of iatrogenesis—that is, illness caused by physicians."

In addition, no controlled studies have compared unlicensed practitioners and licensed practitioners in their effects on consumers. As licensing increases, the possibility of making such a comparison is reduced. Moreover, no record exists of the public requesting the licensure of psychologists or counselors, although the public has initiated requests that summer camps be licensed!

Licensure Makes Practitioners More Competent and Better Distributed. As long as there have been shortages of professionals to provide needed services, this rationale for licensing has been frequently cited. Ironically, as is readily understandable given the status and privileges that often accompany a licensed profession, licensing often creates a shortage of professionals among poor and rural populations. Nevertheless, psychologists have legitimately used this argument to support licensing and other forms of recognition for their profession, citing their broader geographic distribution compared with that of psychiatrists; counselors are now citing equally compelling data which show that they are more broadly distributed than psychologists.

The economic and status factors that cause an unlicensed profession to be more broadly distributed seem to be eliminated with licensure. When a group becomes licensed, it gains increased status, privileges, and usually income. As a result, it usually becomes less willing to provide as much service to minorities, the poor, and the rural population. The cost of services also increases after licensure (Hogan, 1979b; Swanson, 1976).

Rogers (1973) also notes that psychology has tended to ignore the contributions of those who are willing to do what the professionals and their graduate schools appear uninterested in doing, that is, serving the poor, the aged, and the minorities. Some professional psychologists and counselors are concerned that any licensing that determines who shall perform tasks such as counseling, testing, and evaluation may prohibit traditional nonprofessionals, paraprofessionals, ministers, and school counselors from performing services that they have provided for many decades. This particular concern is highlighted within the Community Psychology Division of the American Psychological Association (APA), a division which, because of this issue, now has very strong opponents as well as advocates of professional licensing. A special issue of the *Division of Community Psychology Newsletter,* published in the summer of 1979 (vol. 12, no. 3), identifies the many problems that community psychologists face with regard to licensing and accreditation.

Licensure Upgrades the Profession. This argument states that a licensed profession will have more practitioners committed to improving the profession and maintaining its standards and identity.

There are two major rebuttals to this point. First, numerous writers (for example, Matarazzo, 1977; Van Hoose and Kottler, 1977) state that licensing tends to make training curricula and the definitions for service too rigid. "I believe all the helping professions could conceivably benefit greatly if the opinion makers in our respective professions deliberately encouraged the substitution of heterogeneity of educational requirements over the current standardization of same so much in evidence today" (Matarazzo, p. 858). Rogers (1973) maintains that licensure laws freeze a profession in its past image; examinations are often used that are badly dated, and once the policies and/or procedures have been agreed upon, there is a tremendous reluctance to change them to reflect contemporary standards.

Licensure Helps to Define the Profession. According to this argument, licensing allows the profession to define for itself what it shall and shall not do; therefore, the profession will be more independent, since other professions or the courts will not specify its roles and functions.

The rebuttal here is more a citation of past experiences rather than an argument against the concept itself. Because psychology and counseling have been ambiguously and broadly defined, both professions have had difficulty in making consensual definitions in most states; the definitions are the products of compromises. These fragile alliances, of diverse types of psychologists, which have enabled psychology to become a credentialed and licensed field over the past thirty years, are currently threatened as specialty credentialing and licensing become more emphasized (see Chapter Three). Attempts to modify the APA model license document led to extreme divisiveness rather than refined professional definitions ("Council Votes to Scrub Work on State Licensing Standards, Approve Two Divisions," 1979).

Writing on this issue for counselors, Arbuckle (1977, p. 582) states:

> We are still, however, bedeviled by a fragmentation of counselor functions, and this confusion is as evident in the literature today as it was a decade ago. By the middle of the last decade, Sexton (1965) was saying the less we emphasize the psychological, the psychiatric, and anything therapeutic, the better feeling the students will have toward counseling. Two years later Krueger (1967) warned school counselors about the grave effects of taking seriously such terms as "relationship" and "acceptance." In the same year Venn (1967) stated that the counselor must be a teacher on assignment, like a school administrator, not a specialist from another profession working in a school. By 1973 we had progressed to where Haas (1973) told us that teachers will counsel, clerks will

do the paper work, and counselors will train, and in the same year Carroll (1973) felt that the counselor was the vital strategist, consultant and trainer. The next year Pine (1974) stated that it is time to give school counseling away, and two years later Hayes (1975) said that he was proud to be a counselor, and described himself as an articulation, assessment, attendance, guidance, career, employment, financial, follow-up, foreign student, health, placement, referral and research counselor. Looking at even this brief sampling one might well be bewildered in trying to determine just what is meant by "counselor" competencies!

Because of these varying viewpoints, licensing debates usually create more fragmentation than unity.

Another objection to this premise is that, while licensing does indeed prevent other professions and the courts from telling a profession what to do, it incites challenges to that claim, especially when licensing results in exclusive privileges, such as the right to offer certain services or to obtain third-party payments from insurance companies. Indeed, the American Personnel and Guidance Association (APGA) acknowledges that "the issue [of licensing] was forced upon us by aggressive action of state psychology licensure boards when they moved to restrict the practice of qualified counseling psychologists and other counselors. Perhaps it is only coincidental that these restrictions were increased with the advent of third party payments through private federal health insurance, and with a tightening of the economy" (Gazda, 1977, p. 570). Asher (1979), writing in the *American Mental Health Counselors Association Journal,* notes that the entire profession of counseling is threatened by excluding master's degree social workers, counselors, psychologists, and some master's degree marriage counselors from third-party payments. In short, licensing both protects the domain and invites attack on it.

A final objection to this premise is "that such statutes represent external controls of the profession and that the original reasons for the legislation may one day be replaced by quite different reasons. Once a precedent is established, a legislator, for example, could establish the maximum fee for therapeutic services and the profession would be powerless to prevent it" (Van Hoose and Kottler, 1977, p. 125).

General Criticisms. Professional licensing laws have been criticized for the kind of "paternalism" reflected in laws that require motorcyclists to wear helmets; they interfere with the usual practice of a large number of people for the protection of only a few. However, this response raises the question of how much interference the profession should bear in order to save even one client from an incompetent practitioner.

Koocher (1979) further argues that while the advantages of regulation and credentialing have often been mentioned, the potential costs and problems have too often been ignored. After his review of the face validity, context validity, and criterion-related validity of a variety of credentials, he concludes, "In the final analysis, it seems that whatever existing credentials in psychology do measure, they are clearly not highly valid measures of professional competence. . . . Given the current difficulty in refining the construct of competence as it applies to the practice of psychology, it is unlikely that the credentials' validity will soon improve on this score. This does not mean that credentials are useless but that their value is clearly limited and must be kept in perspective" (p. 702).

While proponents of the points just reviewed have argued their cases in many newsletters, letters to editors, and convention presentations, sometimes providing empirical data in support of their viewpoints, it is important to note that no national evaluation has carefully compared the effects on consumers of mental health services provided by licensed practitioners with those provided by practitioners regulated in alternative ways. Many of the persons who have been critical of licensing are not totally against regulation. Rather, they have criticized the type and content of regulations as opposed to regulations per se.

Alternatives to Present Forms of Licensing

Voluntary Certification. As professionals become more aware of the problems in licensing, they are often ready to consider other forms of credentialing, such as voluntary, or nonstatutory, credentialing. Many professionals who have long been involved with licensing have increasingly felt that certification provides a better balance between consumer welfare and professional guild interests. First, certification can gain a much broader consensus on the restriction of the use of title if functions are not restricted, as they are by many licensing laws. Second, certification by professional approval can help the profession to develop its identity, set standards, and provide the benefits that consumers and the profession derive from such standards without evoking the professional divisiveness caused by statutory acts or subjecting professionals to unwanted controlling legislation at a later time (Van Hoose and Kottler, 1977). Cohen (1976) outlines seven alternatives to the present licensing of the health profession, and most of them still allow the profession to control the credentialing process.

        Self-Disclosure. Hogan (1979b) concludes from his five-year study of traditional and nontraditional psychotherapy fields that our present training-based licensing acts should be abolished and replaced by full disclosure of background information research on performance-related training and certification. Gross (1977) provides a more complete description of how self-disclosure can provide regulation that is even more self-determined than nonstatutory professional certification and yet apparently protects the consumer more than current certification acts do. He proposes a self-disclosure system that he believes provides the information necessary for the consumer to choose a therapist or counselor, a service that licensing itself does not provide. A professional disclosure statute has some of the components that are already contained in the Standards for Providers of Psychological Services (see Chapter Seven). It "assumes that accurate information about the service offered by a practitioner is a consumer's best chance of getting what he or she wants and needs and the best protection against harm and exploitation. In effect, it restricts the counselors to doing what they say they will do" (Gross, p. 588). According to Gross, such a statute, enacted by a state legislature, would include nine provisions:

        (1) Disclosure is to be made to prospective clients before any counseling for which a fee may be charged. It

is to be legible, on a printed form, and also posted conspicuously. (2) The fact that disclosure is required must be disclosed, including information about the particular department of state government that oversees the procedure so that a complainant would know to whom a complaint is to be made. (3) A notarized form is filed annually or whenever a change in the statement is made. (4) Additional disclosure forms are necessary for supervisors and employers. (5) Complaints are made to the department of state government that has responsibility for investigation and public hearings. (6) Provision is made for privilege of counselor records during processing of complaints. (7) Judicial review of decisions is made possible. (8) The offense covered by the statute is the willful filing of false or incomplete information. (9) Punishment includes the judgment (in several classes) of "misdemeanor" and the prohibition from practice [p. 588].

Each practitioner would include in the disclosure his or her name; business address and telephone number; philosophy of counseling or therapy; information about the practitioner's formal education, informal education, and association memberships; and fee schedule. In some ways, Gross' self-disclosure may be more stringent than many current certification acts, which protect only the label of *psychologist* or *counselor*; at the same time, his proposal does not have professional groups specifying who shall or shall not perform certain acts.

Such a self-disclosure statute, of course, requires more trust in the consumers' judgment than many proponents of licensing think is justifiable. In addition, this proposal does not prohibit a practitioner who lacks adequate training or competence from offering a service; however, the person may not be a member of a professional organization whose ethical standards require sufficient training and competence. In fact, Gross' proposal does not mention a practitioner's adherence to any ethical standards.

Competence-Based Credentialing. Competence-based credentialing is not at all a new phenomenon, although it seems to have received significant attention in psychology only in recent years. Flexner (1910), the key author of the 1910 Carnegie

report on medical education, discussed what he believed to be
the major pitfall of competence-based evaluation; that is, a person could cram for an examination, pass it, but "in the presence
of a sick person . . . be quite helpless" (p. 169). Flexner, of
course, was arguing that training credentials be part of the evaluation of candidates.

There was considerable discussion at the 1976 and 1977
Psychology Education and Credentialing Conferences about
whether licensure should be based on competence. This discussion did not progress very far, at least in part because of the
weight of tradition, which has placed more value on one's training and performance on the national examination than on an
evaluation of competence. A more telling concern raised by
some of the more forthright participants was that, in determining competence, a psychologist would be least capable of dem-
onstrating his or her uniqueness. That is, specifying uniqueness
as a psychologist by referring to training is far easier than by
referring to competence. A third point, of course, is that we
now have no adequate measures of competence (Hogan,
1979b)—a persuasive, if not completely accurate, argument.
Hogan hopes to establish a center to conduct research on therapy and to experiment with competence-based measures of
practitioner performance.

Several significant efforts are under way to develop competence-based evaluation of psychologists and counselors. In
1976 the Psychology Examining Committee of California called
for the creation of an ad hoc committee to establish an examination system based on performance criteria. Committee members were selected to represent the specialties of industrial-
organizational, experimental, clinical, school, and counseling-
rehabilitation psychology. The committee has written a
forty-two-page report outlining the proposed examination
system and specifying the mandatory and optional tools, skills,
and tasks or problems that these specialty psychologists must
have or be able to perform. (Full copies of the report may be
obtained by writing to Paul Clement, Ph.D., 190 North Oakland
Ave., Pasadena, CA 91101, and remitting $2.30 to cover the ex-
penses of duplication and mailing.) The Board of Professional

Affairs (BPA) of the APA also plans to develop recommendations for licensing examinations in 1980, giving special attention to the development of instruments for assessing competence in professional psychology.

Public Control of Professional Regulations. Consumer groups have increasingly argued for more participation by consumers in the process of regulating professions. Although these requests do not propose substantively different regulations, most present licensing procedures do not involve the public to any significant degree. What form professional regulations would take if control were primarily public rather than professional is unknown. Thus far, representation of consumers on regulation boards has been proportionately small compared with the representation of professions. Gross (1978) notes that even when lay members are added to professional licensing boards, they seem to be co-opted or otherwise made ineffectual. The little research that has been conducted on the effects of lay members on licensing boards has not yielded any significant evidence of their influence on the boards' decisions.

Matarazzo (1977), in his review of higher education, professional accreditation, and licensure, concluded that there has been too much professional incest among people involved in the three groups. Persons active on professional boards are typically interested in professional accreditation or active in higher education and "[fall] naturally into these three at first seemingly disparate roles without evaluating the potential conflict of interests involved" (p. 856). Obviously, with the traditional emphasis on training credentials for licensing, licensing decisions directly benefit higher education. Would persons more independent of higher education and the professions judge professional regulations more objectively?

While lay consumers would clearly bring an important perspective not currently found on many boards and have no conflicts of interest, they do pose certain questions. What do lay persons know about the assessment of credentials and the competence of psychologists? Can a lay person distinguish good treatment from bad treatment? What about the confidentiality of client material? Since many statutory boards also review ethical complaints, complainants would have to release information to lay as well as professional persons. What ethical standards bind lay participants on boards with respect to confidentiality of material to which they have access?

Perspectives of Licensing Boards and Committees

Members of licensing boards and committees might be described as performing an underpaid (or unpaid), time-consuming, thankless task. To the extent that they make applicants happy by applying the criteria flexibly, they make their professional colleagues unhappy with the heterogeneity of those admitted; to the extent that they make their colleagues happy, they leave a trail of frustrated applicants. In either case, the governor, who typically appoints the board members, may experience more grief than expected and wonder whether he made the wrong appointments. Add to that the harassment and legal entanglements that board members often encounter, and one is surprised to find persons volunteering to serve on these boards and committees!

Warnath (1978, p. 53) cites another problem learned from his experience on the Oregon board of examiners of psychologists.

One reality that quickly becomes apparent is that the Board's power to regulate resides primarily in its ability to persuade and exert informal professional pressures. Licensing Boards are notoriously underfunded. . . . What this means to a board is that its functions must be carried on within the limitations of the money it raises through application, licensing and renewal fees. Financial resources may be so tight than a board may have to delay some activity, such as the publication of the annual list of those who are licensed or the examination of applicants, until it receives enough fee money to cover these activities. . . . The practical implication of this situation is that a Board is very much restricted in its ability to force those who are not licensed from engaging in the activities it is theoretically established to police.

Taking action on malpractice complaints proves to be incredibly frustrating, time consuming, and expensive. The Oregon board found local police all too ready to refer such cases to itself because the police had found that prosecuting malpractice suits was extremely unlikely to result in conviction, since clients were often reluctant to appear in court. In those cases that reached the courts, judges and juries tended to give the professional the benefit of any doubt. Warnath (1978, p. 53) concludes, "Those who believe that the establishment of a Board of Examiners will automatically clean out bad practitioners need to think through the full implications of what would be required of a board in time, energy, and financial resources, if even one court case resulted from its attempts to strictly enforce the provisions of a licensing law related to specific practices."

Licensing board and committee members who have had to defend existing licensing legislation before legislators may know all too well the advantages and disadvantages mentioned in this chapter and the legislative pitfalls described in Chapter Six. On the other hand, it is not surprising that licensing board members often become stronger advocates of licensing *after* service on the boards. The senior author of this book was abruptly introduced to the work of a licensing board on his first day of service, when the chairman of the board, faced with a particularly difficult agenda for the day, stated, "This is where we see the dark side of our profession."

The misrepresentations of titles, services, training, and supervision received and the blatant ethical violations that come to the attention of these boards and committees understandably make one favor more stringent qualifications in licensing acts. Of course, what licensing boards, in their struggles with the dark side of the profession, may not see is the unintended effect of more stringent regulations making some persons ineligible to provide services who may well be as professionally competent and ethical as most licensed professionals.

Licensing boards and committees have yet another difficulty that is rarely known by professionals. In many states, governors have great freedom in making appointments to licensing boards, and may even pass over people recommended by relevant professional associations. If licensing board or committee members do not represent the profession, considerable conflict may exist between the board and the profession itself. The licensing board, of course, is in a powerful position to determine policy regarding who can provide services and under what conditions. Unresolved differences between licensing boards and members of the profession may contribute to the possible expiration of legislative acts governing a profession (as occurred recently to the laws governing psychology in South Dakota).

Legislative Challenges to Licensing

Within the last few years, several legislative developments have occurred that could affect all professional licensing laws. The actual effects of these developments are only beginning to be known; what is clear is that they add a degree of instability to all licensing statutes for the immediate future. At least three types of challenges must now be taken up by licensing advocates: sunset legislation, public hearings, and inquiries from such governmental agencies as the Equal Employment Opportunity Commission, the Federal Trade Commission, and newly formed credentialing review commissions.

As of 1979, sunset legislation had begun to have a significant impact on the licensure of all professions; sunset provisions existed in thirty-nine states as of late 1979. "Sunset refers to the legislative review of existing regulatory programs established under state law. Sunset may assume several different forms, such as (a) a periodic, 'zero based' review of the ongoing need for regulation by law, (b) selection of a date by which the regulatory program will terminate unless expressly authorized by the legislature, or (c) the establishment of a statute termination date in the wake of a negative 'fitness' finding. . . . Its considerable appeal lies in its great promise to cut costs and red tape. It can become, as a result, the vehicle for the personal ambitions of politicians at least as much as an exercise in statecraft" ("Sunset Thunder," 1979).

Sunset legislation can affect many professions simultaneously; for example, Florida's 1976 sunset law committed the state government to review the regulation of twenty-five professions. By requiring that the profession review itself and subject itself to public scrutiny, sunset review can make licensure laws more responsive and effective, especially if sufficient time and resources are set aside for a constructive and thorough review. However, recent experiences have brought out the most negative aspects of sunset legislation, that is, giving the professions inadequate opportunities to document the positive aspects of licensing regulations and providing a forum for politicians and members of other professions who have been aggrieved by psychologists.

Due to sunset provisions, the authority to license psychologists was lost in three states in 1979—Florida, South Dakota, and Alaska. Each case involved slightly different struggles. In Florida, where the legislation required doctoral training in programs of psychology, as compared with the "primarily psychological" training stipulated in many other states, many individuals who were denied licensure because of this more rigid requirement voiced their opposition to the continuance of the licensure law. These vocal opponents were joined by many persons with master's degrees in psychology, who were also ineligible for independent practice in psychology under Florida's legislation.

South Dakota's situation was quite the opposite, in that the state psychological association itself, "after considerable anguish and soul searching, . . . decided to support sunset after a string of examining board actions extended licensure to individuals with questionable training and expertise in psychology. When criticism of the board's actions spilled over into public forum, the board went so far as to threaten its psychologist critics with suspension of their licenses" ("Sunset Thunder," 1979).

In Alaska, a poor performance audit combined with limited state funds resulted in a termination of licensing for psychologists, physicians, and dentists.

California, Oklahoma, and Kansas have all narrowly escaped having their laws expire in a sunset review. Kansas again faces a sunset review in 1980, as does Colorado. Both Pennsylvania and Montana are scheduled for sunset legislation in 1981. The list of states for sunset review in 1982 and thereafter is growing continually as more state legislatures adopt sunset provisions. The BPA of the APA (address in appendix) maintains a list of when states face sunset provisions and whether any organized opposition is known to exist. State psychological associations that would like to be prepared are advised to begin discussion now about how they can make their best case to the public and to legislators for licensing regulations.

Concerns about sunset legislation have prompted the BPA to recommend that the APA assist state licensing boards facing sunset, for example, by providing models for effectively organizing resources to insure productive lobbying and by distributing lists of techniques, communications, and arguments that other states have found useful in professional psychology (Korman, 1973). These materials are similar to those that the APGA has prepared for counselors to promote licensing bills (see Chapter Five).

The BPA (American Psychological Association, Committee on State Legislation, 1979) also takes the position that the psychology law should apply to other groups seeking licensure, urging that requests from marriage and family counselors, social workers, and other counseling groups to be included in the psychology laws or in an omnibus law be denied. The BPA believes that psychology licensing boards should seek to become a part of medical licensing acts rather than of mental health licensing acts.

For states where regulations have expired due to sunset, the effects are not yet obvious. In Florida there was a great deal of media coverage, especially because it became possible for virtually anyone to go out and buy an occupational license as a psychologist. Attempts to license a dog as a psychologist led the Clearwater city commissioners to change city laws and make occupational licensing requirements more strict (Blum, 1979). Other jurisdictions in Florida rapidly changed their own rules to prevent mass purchases of psychologist licenses. The Florida Psychological Association reinstated nonstatutory certification, which was automatically granted to all psychologists previously licensed in Florida; new applicants are asked to complete the standardized examination for professional practice in psychology and to meet other requirements established by the Florida Psychological Association certification committee. The National Register of Health Service Providers in Psychology (see Chapter Eight) has assured states whose licensing authority has expired due to sunset that it will continue to process persons receiving recognized nonstatutory certification. Whether psychologists who have lost state licensing because of sunset legislation will remain eligible for reimbursement of mental health services covered by medical insurance companies is unclear. It is also unclear whether the American Association of State Psychology Boards (AASPB) will permit the national psychology examination to be used in states that have done away with licensing laws; AASPB executives do not want to be perceived as giving approval for such actions (Foltz, 1979).

While the media play of the situation in Florida in many ways had a positive effect on the public's belief that some sort of control was needed for the use of title, just how restrictive any new legislation will be remains to be seen. The restrictiveness will probably be related to how much significant harm unlicensed practitioners cause their clients. Without such information, consumer advocate groups, as well as legislators, may ask whether statutory licensing is necessary.

Public hearings are a second trend that has increased the number of challenges to licensing laws. An increasing number of states are requiring such hearings before legislators can consider the adoption of licensing laws. Moreover, consumer advocate groups are attending these hearings. Such public hearings do give individuals whose thinking may be different from that of the professional organization that developed the proposal the opportunity to state their concerns and objections and to modify the proposal. While these hearings seem logical and reasonable, they do require licensing advocates to be prepared to deal with the public's concerns as well as legislators' concerns. "Dirty linen" among professional groups, often partially concealed from legislators and totally concealed from the general public, may well get aired in public hearings.

Governmental agency inquiries into licensing constitute a third challenge. Such inquiries have come from the Federal Trade Commission, the Equal Employment Opportunity Commission, the Subcommittee on Health Manpower Credentialing of the Department of Health, Education, and Welfare (HEW), and the National Commission for Health Certifying Agencies (NCHCA). In recent years, the Federal Trade Commission has raised questions when it has perceived that organizations' licensing and credentialing activities lead to a restriction of trade. The recent loosening of advertising standards for physicians and lawyers was in part a result of inquiries and actions by the Federal Trade Commission. The commission is on record as indicating that it will be "watchful" of attempts to use state regulatory methods as a cover under which professions can develop and maintain constraints that limit consumers' choices and information (Sweeney and Witmer, 1977).

Another federal agency that has already had an impact on credentialing is the Equal Employment Opportunity Commission, which has been especially concerned with the relationship between credentialing and competence. Do licensing and credentialing operations require employment tests that discriminate against minorities who might actually perform on the job quite satisfactorily? Mackin (1976) reports some of the challenges in this area and predicts that in the future, before tests can be used as a primary criterion for credentialing, a significant relationship will have to be shown between the test results and a person's actual competence and job performance. The Civil Service Commission has raised similar questions.

Two more federal groups are concerned with credentialing in the health field, and they may have significant impact on counseling and psychology: the HEW Subcommittee on Health Manpower Credentialing and the new NCHCA, which was developed under federal aegis. At present neither group has captured the interest of or had major impact on mental health organizations. However, since the federal government now requires certification in a great many professions in order for practitioners to receive financial reimbursement (Mackin, 1976), this committee and commission could be of great significance if they develop policies and standards for credentialing that differ from present ones. As one example, Foltz (1979) notes that the NCHCA is decidedly in favor of certifying rather than licensing.

Furthermore, a National Center for the Study of Professions has been created to conduct studies and programs on competence assessment and licensing in professions. The center is a nonprofit research and information organization that intends to decrease the number of restrictions on gaining entry to occupations and professions, especially where such restraints may be unwarranted, discriminatory, or arbitrary ("Unit to Study Licensing," 1978). The center will examine the possible self-serving motives behind certain professional licensure as well as the social and economic costs and effects of professional policies and practices. Reports from such a center will very likely become documentation in cases for or against licensing.

In summary, as stated at the beginning of this section, what is probably most predictable is that there will be a fair degree of *instability* in licensing laws in several states in the coming years. Therefore, those satisfied or unsatisfied with their present state regulations should be watchful of the status of their own state laws. Chapter Six will provide information and recommended procedures for working with legislatures to develop equitable licensing regulations.

3

Licensing
of Psychologists

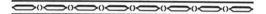

While certification and licensing have become topics of concern
to psychologists only in recent years, consideration of licensing
in psychology extends back nearly to psychology's beginnings.
Cattell lamented in 1937, at the fiftieth anniversary of the
founding of the American Psychological Association (APA),
that he had been concerned with certification ever since the
1890s but that the APA had not found the topic worth studying (Cattell, 1937). The first state to license psychologists was
Virginia in 1946. By 1978, all fifty states, the District of
Columbia, and seven provinces of Canada had established registration, certification, or licensing regulations (Alaska, Florida,
and South Dakota are, as of 1979, without regulations because
licensing regulations reviewed under sunset legislation were not
renewed). Each state, of course, has its own history of licensing.
An inviting task for a sociologically oriented psychohistorian
would be to examine state licensing histories and determine
why diverse states like Connecticut and Virginia were the first
to enact legislation regulating psychologists while equally
diverse states like Missouri, South Dakota, and Vermont were

the last. The two groups most involved at the national level in the development and establishment of licensing and certification regulations are the APA Committee on State Legislation and the American Association of State Psychology Boards (AASPB). The early history of licensing in psychology is best understood by studying the development of these groups.

A Committee on Legislation was established in the APA in the early 1950s. Model state legislation for regulating the practice of psychology was developed by the committee and approved by the APA in 1955. "The 1955 guidelines recommended (a) use of licensure (that is, the regulation of both title and practice) in preference to certification (that is, the regulation of title only), (b) the establishment of the doctorate and at least one year and preferably two years of experience as the basic requirements for entry into the independent professional practice of psychology, (c) the generic approach to licensure (that is, the use of a single license basic to all practices of psychology), and (d) the inclusion of reference to a code of ethics in the law. The 1955 guidelines stood for 12 years, and served through the addition of 32 laws to the 9 previously in existence" (Report of the Committee on State Legislation, 1978).

A 1967 revision provided more details concerning statutory language and covered many more issues relating to the regulation of professional practice. As Hogan (1979b) notes, the relationship between psychology and medicine in 1967 seemed more conducive to dealing with the regulation of practices; the very strong objections by psychiatrists to the licensing of psychologists in the 1950s seemed to have abated. The greatest number of psychologist licensing laws (sixteen) were passed between 1965 and 1969.

The history of psychology licensing in the 1960s is most clearly seen in the development of the AASPB, which was founded in 1961 primarily to cope with the problems encountered by psychologists who moved to different states having differing criteria for licensing or certification.

Coordination was needed to insure some approximation of uniformity in standards and procedures. . . .

On November 19-20, 1959, an historic meeting was held in Chicago under the sponsorship and financial support of the APA Board of Professional Affairs Committee on Examination Procedures. . . . . The American Association of State Psychology Boards formally came into being on August 31, 1961, at the time of the 69th APA convention held in New York City. . . . Membership was to be held by state boards with no distinction between those that were statutory and those that were not. . . . Moves to negotiate reciprocity agreements between concerned boards were anticipated. In subsequent annual meetings, as well as in Executive Committee meetings, formal procedures, and some progress, in arriving at reciprocity agreements were repeatedly discussed. Despite the urgency, results were slow in coming. The states to which, and from which, any appreciable number of psychologists might be expected to move turned out to be rather unpredictable. Likewise, the labor and expense of working out any significant number of details in view of the uncertain numbers of transferring psychologists made widespread agreements unprofitable [Carlson, 1978, pp. 486-488].

In addition to dealing with reciprocity, the AASPB soon became significantly involved in two other areas: (1) legal issues dealing with the relations between state psychological associations and the state psychology examining boards and (2) the development of a national examination. The former issue led to the 1964 publication of a manual on legal issues, which was revised in 1976 (full references for these documents may be found in Carlson, 1978). An AASPB newsletter was begun in 1966 to provide information to individual board members and various boards. The newsletter and periodic flyers provide the most current information of national scope about changes being considered or effected in state licensing laws, court challenges, and the national exams. The AASPB Executive Committee has taken an increasingly visible role in developing national positions on issues concerning professional education and credentialing, such as the licensing of counseling psychologists (American Psychological Association, Division of Counseling

Psychology, 1977). The board has actively promoted the adoption of the guidelines developed in the 1977 Psychology Education and Credentialing Conference (discussed later in this chapter); as of early 1979, twenty-two states had adopted them.

The AASPB Committee on Examination Procedures responded to interest in a professional examination for psychology. An Examination for Professional Practice in Psychology (EPPP) was developed and first issued in 1964 under the auspices of the Professional Examination Service, with minimal financial backing from the AASPB. As of early 1979, every state except Arizona had used or planned to use the EPPP. The test is now in its seventh revision; the test itself, its development, and planned validation studies are described at the end of the next chapter.

Recent Developments

Most of the issues that the APA Committee on State Legislation and the AASPB have worked on have not been readily resolved in the last twenty years. Moreover, issues that were of some concern to a minority of psychologists twenty years ago have become significant concerns to a much larger number as more psychologists have begun to provide psychotherapeutic services and have found that opportunities for service and, even more importantly, reimbursement from medical insurers are increasingly related to licensure status.

As Congress has considered national health insurance more seriously, tension, especially between psychiatrists and psychologists, has increased over which profession will be eligible for reimbursement: "Watch for a decidedly uncivil war to break out among psychiatrists and psychologists and social workers" (Hogan, 1979a, p. A-23). "With the market shrinking, psychiatrists are trying to edge out their non-medical brethren—the psychologists" (Levin, 1979, p. 52). These quotes make clear the genuine concerns psychologists have for maintaining their livelihood. As psychologists seek to define their domain of practice and achieve licensure, counselors have, in turn, felt the beginning of yet another uncivil war. According to Hogan

(1979b), fifteen states consider counseling as part of psychology. Understandably, psychologists, counselors, and other professionals have taken adamant positions in response to recent developments by both the APA Committee on State Legislation and the two conferences held in 1976 and 1977 on the education and credentialing of psychologists. Because of the major impact that these developments are having on counselors and psychologists, each is carefully reviewed.

   Committee on State Legislation. In 1977, the Committee on State Legislation revised the model licensing bill to address (1) the need for more accountability in the quality and appropriateness of service provided the public and (2) the problem of variable standards across states. The three basic principles guiding the revision were as follows:

> First and foremost, and overriding all other considerations, is the concept of protection of the public interest. . . . The second basic principle that has guided the Committee is that psychology is fundamentally a unitary field, and that the practice of psychology, however varied, must be based upon the core body of knowledge that shapes the psychologist's understanding of human problems and his/her specialized practice skills. . . . The third basic principle . . . has been that of protecting the knowledge generation and teaching prerogatives of psychologists. It is the Committee's intent that statutes enacted or amended on the basis of these guidelines shall not interfere with legitimate research and teaching functions of psychologists or the continued diverse development of the field in both its basic and applied aspects [Report of the Committee on State Legislation, 1978].

In contrast to the earlier model, this model for legislation covered all psychological services other than teaching and research services whether offered for a fee or in an institutional setting.

   In 1978, the committee circulated its draft to pertinent boards and committees of national and state psychological organizations. The draft elicited very strong reactions. Given the intent of the model license to cover people in institutional as well as private settings, and an expanded definition of what was included in the practice of psychology, many psychologists suddenly realized that thousands of psychologists not previously licensed would have to be licensed in order to maintain their present employment. Numerous individuals as well as several boards within the APA indicated that they could not support the proposed document.

Throughout 1979, the board of directors of the APA worked diligently to establish compromise definitions of practice that might make the document more acceptable to all professionals within psychology. However, by the time the statement was sufficiently revised to ease the concerns of psychologists who were not involved in mental health services, it was no longer acceptable to licensing proponents. The board had proposed that licensing be limited to psychologists providing direct ameliorative services to individuals and groups and that unlicensed persons be permitted to use the title *psychologist,* since such persons do not provide services and therefore cannot harm the public. Licensing proponents stated that (1) difficulties in defining who was and who was not providing ameliorative services and (2) the use of the title *psychologist* by both licensed and unlicensed persons would create more confusion and divisiveness than the 1967 model guidelines.

Obviously, in seeking to satisfy one group of constituents, another group had been alienated. Consequently, the Council of Representatives of the APA voted at its August 1979 meeting to take no action on the proposed model guidelines. This essentially leaves the APA with the 1967 guidelines still in effect. "The council resolution on the issue in part acknowledged that a professional consensus on statutory practices affecting psychology may be a long way off" ("Council Votes to Scrub Work on State Licensing Standards, Approve Two Divisions," 1979).

In order to give the reader some perspective on the material that led to this impasse, selected definitions and statements from the 1978 model guidelines for state legislation are presented below. These selections are from the draft that appeared before the board of directors, who attempted to modify it to make it more acceptable to traditionally unlicensed psychologists.

A person represents himself/herself to be a psychologist if that person uses any title or description of services incorporating the words "psychology," "psychological," "psychologist," or other terms implying training, experience, or expertise in psychology or offers to render, or renders the services defined as the practice of psychology in this act to individuals, groups, organizations, institutions, or the public.

The practice of psychology within the meaning of this act is defined as, but not limited to, the rendering to individuals, groups, organizations, institutions, or to the public any nonresearch and nonteaching service involving the application of principles, methods, and procedures of understanding, predicting, and influencing behavior, such as principles pertaining to learning, perception, motivation, thinking, emotions, mind-body relationships, interpersonal relationships, and intergroup relationships such as methods and procedures including but not restricted to: interviewing, consulting, the administering, and/or interpreting of tests of mental abilities, aptitudes, interests, opinions, attitudes, emotions, motivations, personality characteristics, and psychophysiological characteristics; the assessment or diagnosis and treatment of emotional, and/or mental, and/or nervous disorder or dysfunction, and/or group dysfunction; psychotherapy; behavior modification; behavior therapy; bio-feedback techniques; hypnosis, marriage, education, and vocational counseling; personnel selection, counseling, and management; evaluation, planning, and consulting for effective work and learning situations, social relationships, organizational development, and group dynamics; and the resolution of interpersonal, intergroup, and social conflicts.

Psychologists who are primarily employed in teaching and/or research but who also engage in the writing or editing of scholarly manuscripts, the presentation of invited lectures and testimony, and research consultation shall be exempt from the provisions of this act for those activities. Nothing in this section shall be interpreted to exempt such an individual if that person renders other professional services as a psychologist.

Applicants for licensure shall possess a doctoral degree from a regionally accredited institution, provided that the degree is obtained from an integrated program of graduate study in psychology as defined by the rules and regulations of the licensing board.

Applicants for licensure shall possess at least one year of supervised experience. The board shall promulgate criteria defining the circumstances under which supervised experience shall qualify the candidate for licensure. The supervision requirements may be waived by the board at its discretion for an individual who has demonstrated excellence in psychology by past achievements.

At the end of each registration period the psychologist must submit to the board satisfactory proof that the required continuing education experience specified in the rules and regulations of the board has been successfully completed.

The board shall consist of two public members and five psychologists representing different specialties. The psychologist members shall be appointed from a list of nominees submitted by the state psychological association [Report of the Committee on State Legislation, 1978].

Given the controversial nature of these stipulations, it is unlikely that psychologists will agree in the near future to formulate an APA-endorsed model licensing bill. Without such a national standard, states might develop increasingly different regulations. While no national document from either the APA or the AASPB would be binding on state legislatures, the existence of such a document would help make state licensing acts more similar.

Because of the breadth of the APA proposed definition of psychological services, counselors have expressed concern over the degree of overlap between professions. Both counselors and psychologists must remain as informed as possible about the actions of their state and national organizations with respect to licensing acts, since definitions can easily be rewritten in ways that would significantly affect the careers of many thousands of persons.

Education and Credentialing in Psychology, 1976 and 1977 Conferences. Other significant developments in licensing and credentialing on the national level occurred in two meetings held in 1976 and 1977. These meetings stimulated changes in state laws, APA accreditation criteria, and the standards of eligibility for such nonstatutory credentials as the National Register of Health Service Providers in Psychology and the American Board of Professional Psychology.

The problems that were cited as prompting these meetings were the following:

a. The diverse standards and criteria for the licensing/certification of psychologists by the 51 State Boards of Examiners of Psychology across the country. b. Court challenges to the existing definitions of the title and practice of psychology in a number of jurisdictions. c. Emerging public and federal concerns related to the credentialing and licensure of all professions and proposals for their regulation. d. The emergence of new education and training models for the preparation of professional psychologists, and their relationship to the APA accreditation system (for example, Professional Schools, Psy. D. degrees). e. The absence of educational standards for Civil Service (federal, state, and local) classifications and designations of psychologists. f. The proliferation of educational programs which purport to educate psychologists outside of Departments of Psychology or Schools of Psychology, most of which are not accredited by the APA. g. The lack of articulation between the educational and credentialing components of the field. h. The issue of competency. It is not clear to what extent quality graduate education produces consistently competent graduates, and this is of great concern to consumers, licensing boards, and training programs themselves. i. The lack of a national standard to define a Doctorate in Psychology. j. Concern with a national health policy [Wellner, 1978, p. 1].

The 1976 conference was attended by thirty-nine invited participants representing such groups as the AASPB, various APA boards, and the councils of directors of clinical, counseling, and internship settings. No APA division representatives were invited. Most participants were primarily clinical psychologists. Participants were provided with the *Sourcebook* (1976), which included relevant APA documents (standards, criteria for accreditation, and so on), the current status of several important court cases, data on the various state licensure and certification laws, the National Academy of Science (Commission on Human Resources, 1975) survey of doctorates granted (2,587 in all fields of psychology versus 753 in guidance and counseling), data from the *National Register* that showed licensed applicants who had received thirty-five different graduate degrees (for example, J.D., M.P.H., and Th.D.) from thirty-five different departments; the APA Division of Counseling Psychology's statement on the licensing and credentialing of counseling psychologists (American Psychological Association, Division of Counseling Psychology, 1975) and the American Personnel and Guidance Association model for state legislation. Obviously, this material focused the discussion on the problems created by counselors, counseling psychologists, or "whoever they are getting all those crazy degrees in departments that wouldn't know a psychologist if they saw one" (in the words of one of the participants). The other salient issue was "diploma mills"—schools not regionally accredited but authorized in various states to give degrees that seem to allow holders to represent themselves as psychologists to licensing boards.

In the *Sourcebook* (1976), a paper by Berger presented some highlights from a survey concerning the eligibility rules for the licensing examination. Berger concluded that the term "primarily psychological in nature" is a euphemism for "not psychology." Highlights of the findings from the survey were the following:

1. 95 percent of the states require a doctoral degree. Of those, 18 percent require that the doctorate must be a Ph.D.

2. One third of the states do not require that the degree be from a university which is regionally accredited.

3. 95 percent of the states responding indicated that they have a requirement that the program be "primarily psychological in nature." There is no consistency on how Boards define or handle the phrase "primarily psychological in nature." It ranges from a literal interpretation of a major in psychology to a program in any major field as long as there are at least 30 credits in psychology.

4. 63 percent of the states with a requirement of "primarily psychological" interpret this to mean a major field in psychology. The major field in psychology is also very loosely interpreted and includes a range of definitions.

5. 76 percent of the states indicate that they have a requirement specifying a minimum number of credits in psychology. This can be in terms of specified number of credit hours or a percentage of the total number of graduate courses.

6. 29 percent of the sample indicated that there was a requirement for a dissertation that was psychological.

7. About 5 states indicate that they use APA approval as a standard for evaluating the educational credentials [*Sourcebook,* 1976].

This information did help emphasize some of the difficulties encountered by persons licensed in one state who move to another. Despite equivalent laws, the interpretation of "primarily psychological in nature" varies greatly.

Berger further warned that, in the long run, departments of psychology may suffer because of the potential growth of marginally adequate programs both within and outside university settings. "Flexibility of standards may be undermining education in psychology by cheap programs driving the quality programs off the market" (Wellner, 1976, p. 28).

The steering committee for the conference presented six key questions for the group's discussion:

1. Can we identify and agree on a basic *academic core* for the training of psychologists at the doctoral level, recognizing the values of fostering innovation and experimentation?

2. Can the APA Accreditation Criteria (and other APA policy statements, for example, COSL, Standards, and so on) and state Licensing/Certification Boards agree on what makes a program *"psychological"* or *"primarily psychological in nature?"*

3. Can we proceed to strengthen our profession and identity by *using common language* (definitions, criteria, and so on) in *policy statements, legislative proposals, standards,* and so on? How do we implement that goal if, indeed, it is a desirable one?

4. How can we deal with emerging national concerns and developments and recognize *states' rights* on credentialing and licensing issues?

5. How can we enhance appropriate communications between University training programs and Licensing/Certification Boards, given *academic freedom values* and legislative intent to *protect the public?*

6. How do we improve the general communications among psychology organizations to assure *continuing open dialogue* and *appropriate feedback* in policy formations and implementation [Wellner, 1976, p. 32]?

Four task forces working on these issues produced several sets of recommendations; two or more of these task forces developed proposals to establish a national review commission, to require that academic preparation in psychology be provided in psychology departments or in integrative programs that meet APA standards, and to establish a national set of minimal educational standards for licensing and credentialing in psychology. The task force working on basic professional education had as its first principle: "Basic professional education in psychology must be obtained within an integrative program of psychology offered by a department of psychology or professional school of psychology located in a regionally accredited educational institution" (Wellner, 1976, p. 43).

When these task force reports and proposals were distributed at the 1976 APA convention, counseling psychologists expressed the most dismay (psychologists other than clinical and counseling psychologists were not well represented at the 1976 meeting; therefore, few psychologists outside of those groups were aware of the 1976 meeting's recommendations.) While the reports were issued only as information and were not binding on anyone, the threat felt by many counseling psychologists was real. Over half the persons who identify themselves as counseling psychologists did not receive degrees from psychology departments. The degree of alarm expressed by many counseling psychologists led to the creation of a blue ribbon panel, which was to have further discussions regarding these issues primarily with the AASPB.

A meeting between this panel and AASPB representatives was held in early 1977. "The meeting produced a statement of understanding between Division 17 [the APA Division of Counseling Psychology] and the AASPB. It was apparent that the very diverse constituency of Division 17 meant that the division could not and would not encourage or otherwise support the application for licensing or certification by all its constituent members. There was a very quick consensus that once a definition is arrived at on professional education in psychology and once it is clear that such education can occur in educational units outside the department of psychology, many of the issues were reduced if not eliminated" (*Sourcebook II*, 1977, pp. 11-12).

The recommendations of the 1976 Education and Credentialing meeting led to a second meeting in 1977, which had the following explicit objectives: (1) to develop a set of recommendations for the APA Council of Representatives and other relevant groups on the definition and core elements of professional education in psychology; (2) to develop recommendations on mechanisms to guide, monitor, and appropriately integrate the education and credentialing aspects of the field, and (3) to develop a plan of action for following through on the first two objectives.

For the 1977 conference, in addition to the groups represented in 1976, *all* APA divisions were invited to attend; eighteen participated. While division representatives were added to this second conference, the thirteen-member steering committee for the conference and the continuing followup activities has never had a member who was trained or currently functioning as a counseling psychologist, a rehabilitation psychologist, or an industrial psychologist—to name just a few of the concerned specialists (Bartlett, 1979).

The conference participants again worked in task forces with periodic plenary sessions. The recommendations below represent the results of many hours of compromise among the task forces. These compromises did not by any means elicit unanimous support, but they were approved by at least a simple majority of the conference's fifty participants, who represented various professional organizations and APA divisions and boards.

Most important to many concerned industrial-organizational, developmental, school, and counseling psychologists was the inclusion in the definition of a psychology program of the statement "The program, *wherever it may be administratively housed,* must be clearly identified and labeled as a psychology program" (emphasis added). This part of the definition allows programs to be recognized that are not housed in psychology departments or schools of psychology. The full set of criteria is reproduced below. (Between August 1977 and December 1978, these criteria were adopted by the licensing boards of twenty-two states as a definition of a psychology program. The full rationale for each of these criteria may be found in Wellner, 1978, pp. 31-40).

1. Programs that are accredited by the American Psychological Association are recognized as meeting the definition of a professional psychology program. The criteria for accreditation serve as a model for professional psychology training.

2. Training in professional psychology is doctoral training offered in a regionally accredited institution of higher education.

3. The program, wherever it may be administratively housed, must be clearly identified and labeled as a

psychology program. Such a program must specify in pertinent institutional catalogues and brochures its intent to educate and train professional psychologists.

4. The psychology program must stand as a recognizable, coherent organizational entity within the institution.

5. There must be a clear authority and primary responsibility for the core and specialty areas whether or not the program cuts across administrative lines.

6. The program must be an integrated, organized sequence of study.

7. There must be an identifiable psychology faculty and a psychologist responsible for the program.

8. The program must have an identifiable body of students who are matriculated in that program for a degree.

9. The program must include supervised practicum, internship, field, or laboratory training appropriate to the practice of psychology.

10. The curriculum shall encompass a minimum of three academic years of full time graduate study. In addition to instruction in scientific and professional ethics and standards, research design and methodology, statistics, and psychometrics, the core program shall require each student to demonstrate competence in each of the following substantive content areas. This typically will be met by including a minimum of three or more graduate semester hours (5 or more graduate quarter hours) in each of these 4 substantive content areas: a) biological bases of behavior: physiological psychology, comparative psychology, neuropsychology, sensation and perception, psychopharmacology. b) cognitive-affective bases of behavior: learning, thinking, motivation, emotion. c) social bases of behavior: social psychology, group processes, organizational and systems theory. d) individual differences: personality theory, human development, abnormal psychology.

In addition to these criteria, all professional education programs in psychology will include course requirements in specialty areas [Wellner, 1978, pp. 29-30].

The other major accomplishment of the 1977 conference was a proposal for a national commission, which would designate doctoral programs in psychology:

It is proposed that there be established a National Commission for the Designation of Doctoral Programs in Psychology. This would be an independently incorporated Commission whose composition would include representatives of the following organizations: The American Psychological Association Board of Directors, the Council of University Directors of Clinical Psychology, the Council of Directors of Counseling Psychology Training Programs, the Council of Directors of School Psychology Programs, the Council of Graduate Departments of Psychology, the National Council of Schools of Professional Psychology, the APA Board of Professional Affairs, the APA Education and Training Board, the Council for the National Register of Health Service Providers in Psychology, and the American Association of State Psychology Boards. The Commission would also have at least one member serving as a representative of the public interest.

The Commission's function would be that of certifying whether doctoral programs conformed with the criteria of a "psychology program," as defined by the Conference on Education and Credentialing in Psychology. Two points should be emphasized with respect to the Commission's function: (1) Certification by the Commission would not have any implications concerning the quality of the program offered or the competencies of its graduates. (2) The operation of the Commission is not intended to supplant the current accreditation procedures of the APA.

The Commission is seen as serving three important functions: (1) it would provide State Boards of Examiners with an unambiguous basis for deciding whether the program of study followed by an applicant for licensure or certification constituted a psychology program. (2) It would allow students to determine whether a particular program of studies constituted a psychology program such that it would generally make them eligible to apply for examination by a State Board of Examiners. (3) The Commission, by virtue of its composition, would provide an established channel of communication between the licensing/certification and service providing communities on the one hand and the education and training committees on the other [Wellner, 1977, p. 33].

After the 1977 meeting, the steering committee worked out the details of a proposal for such a commission, its relationship to current professional organizations, and a proposed budget. These details may be found in what is now known as "the blue book" (Wellner, 1978).

Throughout 1978 and early 1979, this proposal was carefully considered by various boards and committees of the APA, councils of training directors, and departmental chairpersons. Numerous questions and issues were raised, especially since the proposed commission would be independent of the APA, put significant constraints on the academic curriculum, and require financial commitments from all universities and organizations wishing to be recognized. In responding to these concerns, the APA Council of Representatives asked that the board of directors supervise at least a year of in-house study at APA of the proposed commission. While urging that the designation system be developed within the APA, the council also suggested that a consortium of groups outside of the APA should implement the system "unless the task force experience provides overriding reasons for a different implementing system" ("Council Votes to Scrub Work on State Licensing Standards . . . ," 1979, p. 7).

Implementing a designation system would primarily affect the programs that are not now labeled psychology programs but that graduate persons who consider themselves psychologists and apply for credentials as psychologists (especially counseling, human development, family services, and industrial-organization programs). These programs would have to meet the criteria of the designation system lest their graduates be summarily declared ineligible for licensing as psychologists. The intent of many persons proposing the designation

system is to reduce the problems resulting from the requirement
in most state licensing laws that the educational background be
psychological or "primarily psychological in nature." The designation system would declare unambiguously that the program
either was or was not a psychology-based program. Designation
is different from accreditation (see Chapter Seven) in that accreditation requires meeting a number of quality requirements,
while designation requires meeting only specific formal structures and course categories.

As with the model licensing bill, there are many strongly
held views about the proposed commission. At this point,
whether sufficient consensus can be reached to implement such
a commission in the near future is unclear. While some opponents object that the proposal seems to overspecify the content
areas of psychological training, other opponents argue that the
proposal would weaken already inadequate standards for such
training.

Psychology's Perennial Issue: Master's-Level Licensing

The role of the master's degree holder has been controversial in professional psychology since World War II. Only at
that point did professional psychology become led predomi-
nantly by doctoral-level psychologists. Controversies about
whether master's-level psychologists should be licensed have
continued for over thirty years now. Woods (1971) found APA
documents from 1947 and 1948 noting: "It is important that
this training be obtained under psychological auspices and such
[master's-level] persons shall work in association with or under
the supervision of psychologists. It is likely that some kinds of
psychological work in clinics will always be performed by persons with less than doctoral training. Many clinical programs
will require psychological workers who serve as assistants or
technicians under supervision of the clinical psychologist. For
these assistants, the master's degree is appropriate" (Woods, p.
704).

Moore (1954) reviewed surveys taken and discussions
held at regional conventions in 1952 and 1953 on "What should

be the nature and purpose of the master's degree in psychology?" Concern was expressed over three relatively different types of master's programs whose goals were radically different but whose graduates could all apply for positions or credentialing designed for master's-degree holders: (1) programs with a general theoretical major, (2) programs of general theoretical nature designed for students seeking the doctorate but providing, by means of additional courses, some professional training for students who seek only master's degrees, and (3) programs oriented primarily toward professional training of various types.

McTeer (1952) concluded from a survey of courses and jobs for master's-degree holders that the technical training at the master's level had expanded tremendously in the preceding decade. He went on to say, "The real question becomes that of the association's attitude toward people with this level of training specialization. Are we going to find a way to keep these people identified with the profession and therefore subject to our ethics and professional disciplines? Or, are we to let them slip off into fragmented 'specialty societies' to devise their own codes and ethics independently of those now being structured by the American Psychological Association?" (McTeer, p. 19). Remember, this was 1952!

Woods's (1971) article summarizes the major actions of APA regarding petitions from one part of the organization to give more recognition to master's-degree holders. These petitions have always been countered by other parts that have generally succeeded in keeping the status quo—master's-degree holders being perceived as below the journeyman level, requiring supervision by doctoral-level psychologists, and not being admitted to full voting membership in the APA.

In the past decade, the Vail Training Conference, at which young and minority-group psychologists had greater representation than at earlier training conferences, firmly recommended increased recognition in professional psychology of master's-degree holders (Korman, 1973). These recommendations, however, were just as firmly opposed by the APA Board of Professional Affairs. Attempts to legitimize training and standards for the master's-degree holder encountered more resistance than ever, especially from clinical psychologists, who preferred that all master's-level professional training be terminated. In 1977, the APA Council of Representatives adopted the following resolution on the issue:

> The title "Professional Psychologist" has been used so widely and by persons with such a wide variety of training and experience that it does not provide the information the public deserves.
>
> As a consequence, the APA takes the position and makes it a part of its policy that the use of the title "Professional Psychologist," and its variations such as "Clinical Psychologist," "Counseling Psychologist," "School Psychologist," and "Industrial Psychologist" are reserved for those who have completed a Doctoral Training Program in Psychology in a university, college, or professional school of psychology that is APA or regionally accredited. In order to meet this standard, a transition period will be acknowledged for the use of the title "School Psychologist," so that ways may be sought to increase opportunities for doctoral training and to improve the level of the educational codes pertaining to the title.
>
> The APA further takes the position and makes part of its policy that only those who have completed a Doctoral Training Program in Professional Psychology in a university, college, or professional school of psychology that is APA or regionally accredited are qualified independently to provide unsupervised direct delivery of professional services including preventive, assessment, and therapeutic services. The exclusions mentioned above pertaining to school psychologists do not apply to the independent, unsupervised, direct delivery of professional services discussed in this paragraph.
>
> Licensed MA psychologists, having met earlier standards of the profession, are to be regarded as comparably qualified through education, experience, examination, and the test of time as are present and future doctoral psychologists and shall be entitled under APA guidelines to hold the title of "psychologist." It is not the intent of this resolution and policy statement to take away any of

their accomplishments or status [Resolution on the Master's Level Issue, 1977].

Readers interested in survey data, standards, and elaborations on psychologists' positions on master's-level training models should consult the *Sourcebook on Master's Level Issues* (American Psychological Association, Office of Educational Affairs, 1977), Autor and Zide (1974), Bullington (1979), and Albee (1977). Innumerable other documents lie within the files and newsletters of the counseling, clinical, and community psychology divisions of APA and of the APA Education and Training Board and Board of Professional Affairs. A dedicated archivist could no doubt fill a bookshelf with what has been written about the master's degree in psychology!

The recent APA position exacerbates rather than resolves this issue, since it effectively excludes master's-level practitioners from independent practice. Cummings (1979) outlines the possible dangers resulting from the disaffection of master's-level psychologists and the infighting created within the profession: "The issue is literally tearing apart many of our state associations. Some, in an attempt at egalitarianism, have admitted master's level candidates to full voting membership, only to be swamped by what is soon a majority demanding that the state's licensing laws be amended downward" (p. 2). With the conflict between master's-level and doctoral-level persons contributing to the sunset of at least one state's licensing (Florida), Cummings is concerned that continuing stresses of this sort may lead to fewer and fewer statutory regulations for psychologists. "If that happens, the inclusion of psychology in national health insurance will be a dead issue . . . . If we do not begin to find solutions to our perennial internal problem, all of our recent gains will vanish and our disaffected master's colleagues will yet see the undoing of clinical psychology" (p. 2).

On the other side, Randolph (1979) cites recent data that most of the service provided by the nation's community mental health centers is delivered by master's-level personnel and that community health center directors have rated master's- and doctoral-level psychologists as about equally competent for that setting. Master's-level social workers and master's-level nurses are both recognized by the National Institute of Mental Health as mental health providers who are qualified to receive support funds for mental health training. However, in psychology, master's-level psychologists have not been granted such formal sanction. The number of persons trained at the master's level in psychology is substantial and continues to grow. *"Graduate Study in Psychology* for 1979-80, published by the APA, lists 222 terminal master's programs in psychology . . . and I am not even speaking to the several hundred more terminal master's programs in related fields whose graduates attempt to identify with psychology. . . . Between 1972 and 1977 . . . these programs produced an estimated 21,000 terminal master's level persons" (Cummings, 1979, p. 2).

The institution of licensing for marriage and family therapists, counselors, and rehabilitation counselors in some states (see Chapter Five) has been partly stimulated by the exclusion of master's-level persons from psychological licensing. Many persons trained in master's-level psychology programs can much more easily obtain (or already have) the credentials for these types of master's-level credentialing as compared to those credentials needed for doctoral-level licensing, given both the time demands and the relatively few places that allow master's-degree holders in psychology to enter doctoral programs in psychology (Cummings, 1979).

Other side effects of the poor relationships between master's- and doctoral-level psychologists can be seen in the current debate between the APA and the National Association of School Psychologists over who should accredit school psychology programs. Since the APA accredits only doctoral-level programs, many school psychologists (most of whom hold master's degrees) have declared their allegiance to the National Association of School Psychologists, which considers master's-level psychologists to be full professionals and which is arguing for the accrediting authority of the National Council for Accreditation of Teacher Education, an agency that will accredit master's-level programs (see Chapter Seven).

With the numbers of master's-level psychologists involved

and the economic realities such as jobs and third-party payments, it is unlikely that this issue will be easily resolved in the near future. In the meantime, persons completing or holding master's degrees in psychology must realize that there is an incredibly strong resistance to giving them full recognition as psychologists. However, doctoral-level psychologists who advocate policies that exclude master's degree holders must acknowledge that many master's-level psychologists have been providing many mental health services in this country for decades and that many more master's-level psychologists continue to enter the job market. Excluding them from licensing will probably heighten public awareness of these long-standing internal debates and possibly contribute, indirectly if not directly, to serious questioning of psychological licensing.

A final note for the reader interested in the few remaining opportunities for licensing as a master's-level psychologist: Most of the issues in qualifying for licensing discussed in Chapter Four apply equally to master's-level as well as doctoral-level persons in those states where master's-level licensing is still provided.

Current Status of State Psychology Statutes

Providing completely up-to-date information on psychology laws is an impossible task; the combination of court challenges, sunset laws, and attempts to revise legislation by professional associations and licensing boards has resulted in almost annual reconsideration of many psychology licensing laws in various states. The summaries of state laws that follow represent the status of legislation as of late 1979. Annually updated versions of this information may be obtained from the APA Office of Professional Affairs (address in appendix). Details of state laws as they existed in early 1978 may be found in Lahman (1978). Lahman compiled information filling a two-inch-thick loose-leaf binder to provide a comprehensive resource for psychologists and others affected by the psychology licensing and certification requirements of the United States and Canada. While his book is the best single resource for the details of state statutes, he appropriately warns, "Please read this book with caution. It is not an official publication sanctioned by any professional organization. . . . Due to the possibility that I may have inaccurately represented some requirements or that they have been modified since inclusion in this publication, I strongly encourage you to contact the appropriate board or organization before making a decision based on the material as presented on the following pages" (Lahman, 1978).

A second major resource for details on the requirements of state statutes is Hogan's *The Regulation of Psychotherapies: A Handbook of State Licensure Laws* (1979b). This book, the second of four volumes covering history, laws, malpractice, and bibliographic resources in the licensing of physicians, psychologists, social workers, and marriage and family counselors, not only provides details on each of the laws but also analyzes how the definitions of each profession either enable or preclude various professionals from practicing psychotherapy in each state. Hogan also notes that over half of all state laws expressly include psychotherapy within the practice of psychology and that the "remainder have definitions of practice so broad that psychotherapy undoubtedly would be included" (p. 8).

In order to make the data on state laws more comprehensible, we have focused on the information that is most important to applicants for licensing, and we have identified the requirements held by the majority of states. (As already noted, as of 1979, Alaska, Florida, and South Dakota are without legislative regulations for psychologists.) In addition to the requirements reviewed here, most states also specify that applicants be of good character, not be engaged in unethical practice, be twenty-one years of age or older, and be or intend to be a citizen of the United States (or Canada).

Doctoral Licensing. Because relatively few states treat doctoral and master's degree applicants similarly, we have separated the review of current status of states' legislative requirements into doctoral- and master's-level sections. As stated in Chapter One, certification, as used by the APA and the present authors, simply protects the use of the title *psychologist,* while licensing laws regulate both the use of the title and define the activities that constitute the practice of psychology. All but thirteen states have licensing acts for doctoral-level psychologists. The thirteen with certification acts are Arizona, Illinois, Indiana, Kansas, Louisiana, Maryland, Mississippi, Nebraska, New Hampshire, New Mexico, New York, Rhode Island, and Wyoming.

Experience required. Most states have professional experience requirements that a person must satisfy to apply for the licensing or certification examination. Many states specify that the experience must take place after receiving the doctorate and completing the internship. Some states also specify that at least part of the experience must be supervised by psychologists licensed in that state or by their equivalents. The states vary considerably, however, as to what constitutes experience. The states require various amounts of postdegree experience and experience under supervision. For simplicity, we will list three major groups: (1) states or provinces with no experience required: Alabama, Arizona, Nebraska, North Dakota, Wyoming, Alberta, Quebec, Saskatchewan; (2) those that require at least one year of experience obtained after receiving the doctoral degree and completing internship (see Table 1); and (3) those that

Table 1. States and Provinces Requiring One or More Years of
Postdegree Experience

California	Massachusetts	Pennsylvania
Colorado	Michigan	Rhode Island
Connecticut	Minnesota	South Carolina
Delaware	Mississippi	Texas
District of Columbia	Missouri	Utah
Idaho	Nevada	Vermont
Indiana	New Hampshire	Virginia
Iowa	New Jersey	Washington
Kansas	New Mexico	West Virginia
Louisiana	North Carolina	Wisconsin
Maryland	Ohio	Ontario

require at least one year of experience to be supervised by licensed psychologists in that state or their equivalent (see Table 2). States and provinces not named may require one or more

Table 2. States and Provinces Requiring Experience Under the Supervision
of Psychologists

California	New Hampshire	Texas
Colorado	New Jersey	Utah
Delaware	New York	Vermont
Idaho	North Carolina	Virginia
Indiana	Ohio	Washington
Iowa	Oregon	West Virginia
Kansas	Pennsylvania	Wisconsin
Louisiana	Rhode Island	British Columbia
Massachusetts·	South Carolina	Ontario
Mississippi		

years of pre- or postdoctoral experience, which need not be
supervised.

Examinations. Every state in the United States except
Michigan requires that a written and/or oral examination be
taken unless the candidate qualifies for exemption because of
licensure in another state (reciprocity) or the holding of a diplomate from the American Board of Professional Psychology.
(Under the law passed in Michigan in 1978, the examining
board will determine whether to make the examination mandatory; that decision had not been made at the time of this writing.) In Canada, examinations are mandatory only in Manitoba,
New Brunswick, and Ontario.

Reciprocity. Reciprocity is complex and unpredictable.
Despite the intentions of the AASPB to make it easier for
psychologists to move to a new state, various state legislatures
have guarded their prerogatives with a variety of stipulations.
While nearly every state will consider reciprocity, most do not
specify the states with which they will maintain reciprocity. In
actual practice, this list changes from year to year as states modify their policies and procedures. In short, being licensed in one
state provides little assurance of being licensed in another state
through reciprocity; each individual must check with the state
in question.

A diplomate from the American Board of Professional
Psychology (ABPP) waives the examination requirement in all
but the following thirteen states: Arizona, Arkansas, Hawaii,

Idaho, Illinois, Kansas, Maine, Missouri, Nebraska, Nevada, Oklahoma, Oregon, and Vermont. Most of these states will consider waiving the examination for ABPP diplomates but do not do so automatically.

Continuing Education. In the early 1970s several states began to require that psychologists, like several other types of licensed health professionals, receive continuing education in order to renew their licenses. Many psychologists supported this development, but surveys of psychologists indicated embarrassingly few professional educational activities among certified psychologists (Brown and Briley, 1979). At the time of this writing, twelve states have a continuing education requirement. These requirements specify certain amounts of time in different categories of activities, such as workshops and instructional seminars, professional meetings and conventions, publication, and self-study. In most states, only a small portion of the total time required can be self-study time. Most statutes stipulate that at least a third of the hours required be spent in instructional workshops or seminars.

In recognition of the interest expressed not only by psychologists in those states requiring continuing education, but also by the growing number of licensed psychologists voluntarily participating in continuing education, the APA approved a sponsor approval system in 1979, which provides guidelines for developing and assessing continuing education programs. By having a national review and listing of approved programs, this system eliminates the inefficiency and confusion that results when sponsors must apply for approval to various states, with each having various guidelines, credit systems, application forms, and schedules. The one problem that many psychologists have found in continuing education requirements is not knowing which programs count for credit. A licensed psychologist who spends over $1000 to attend a specialized assessment workshop that is not approved by the state licensing board will no doubt feel greatly aggrieved.

Master's-Level Licensing. Eighteen states and three Canadian provinces have some sort of licensing or registration for master's-level psychologists. Alaska, Michigan, and South

Dakota also had such opportunities until 1978, but the new Michigan law licenses no new master's-level "psychological examiners" after 1980; South Dakota's and Alaska's licensing acts expired under sunset legislation in 1979. Five states presently permit the independent, unsupervised practice of psychology at the master's level: Iowa, Minnesota, Missouri, Pennsylvania, and West Virginia. In most of these states, more experience is required for licensing at the master's level than at the doctoral level. For master's-level licensure, Iowa requires five years of experience (two supervised); Minnesota, two years postdegree experience; Missouri, three years experience; Pennsylvania, four years postdegree experience (two supervised); and West Virginia, five years postdegree experience, all supervised. A written and/or oral examination is required in all five states. Most of these states and those described in Table 3 also require good character recommendations, not being engaged in unethical practice, being eighteen years or older, and being a U.S. or Canadian citizen or intending to become one. Of the five states with master's-level independent practice, in all but Iowa one is recognized as a psychologist without a qualifying label; in Iowa the term "practice of associate psychology" is used for master's-level licensees.

Thirteen states provide limited licensing or certification of master's-level persons. In all of these states, a title other than *psychologist* is used, such as *psychological associate, psychological examiner,* or a specialty designation such as *educational psychologist* or *school psychologist.* Various stipulations are made as to the functions allowed and/or the supervision by licensed doctoral-level psychologists that is necessary. Table 3 summarizes the titles, experience, and examination requirements in these thirteen states. The number entered under the postdegree experience column indicates the number of years of experience that must be completed after the master's degree is completed. In Oregon, for example, one must have four years of supervised experience (including internship), but all of this could be obtained while completing the degree; in California, however, an educational psychologist needs only three years of experience, but at least two years must occur after the degree is

Table 3. States Providing Limited Licensing or Certification
of Master's-Level Psychologists

| State | Title Covered | Years Experience Required | | | Exami- nation Manda- tory |
		Post- degree	Super- vised	Total	
Arkansas	Psychological Examiner	0	0	0	Yes
California	Educational Psychologist	2	1	3	Yes
	Psychological Assistant	a	a	a	No
Kentucky	Certified for Supervised Practice	a	a	a	Yes
Maine	Psychological Examiner	0	1	1	Yes
New Hampshire	Associate Psychologist	a	a	a	No
North Carolina	Psychological Examiner	0	0	0	Yes
Ohio	School Psychol- ogist	3	3	3	Yes
Oregon	Psychological Associate	0	4	4	Yes
Tennessee	Psychological Examiner	0	0	0	No
Texas	Psychological Associate	0	0	0	No
Vermont	Psychological Associate	3	3	4	Yes
Virginia	School Psychol- ogist	3	3	4	Yes
Wisconsin	School Psychol- ogist	b	b	b	

[a]Continuous supervision required.

[b]See text.

completed. The supervised experience column lists the number of years of experience that must be formally supervised; for example, in Vermont at least three of the four years of pre- or postdegree experience must be supervised.

In Wisconsin, school psychologists can be licensed without fulfilling any requirements beyond possessing the Department of Public Instruction's certification as the highest-level school psychologist. Alberta, British Columbia, and Quebec also register master's-level persons as psychologists without an examination, and only British Columbia requires any supervised experience (one year).

4

Issues and Ambiguities in Requirements for Psychology Licenses

Applicants for licensing in psychology have often found the process fraught with unexpected challenges of their credentials. Eminence of the school granting one's degree is no guarantee of eligibility. In fact, even eminence as a writer or practitioner of psychology does not guarantee eligibility (Hogan, 1979a). This chapter discusses the major difficulties encountered by applicants for certification and licensing and recommends how to enhance one's eligibility.

Many challenges to a person's qualifications have resulted in court cases, which are reviewed to elucidate the type of challenge as well as to describe how the courts act in eligibility suits. Subsequently, several general issues for eligibility are identified and illustrated with case examples. Many of these issues will become more important if a national designation commission, as described in Chapter Three, is established. Special note is made of possible problems in qualifying for licensure that readers may act accordingly. The chapter concludes with a description of the content and proposed modifications of the national Examination for Professional Practice in Psychology (EPPP).

Court Cases

In recent years four persons who considered their training to be in counseling psychology were denied admission to examinations for licensing and challenged these determinations in court. Each of these cases had a different outcome, although the applicants' backgrounds were not very different; therefore, each is discussed separately.

The earliest case was *Coxe* v. *Mississippi Board of Psychological Examiners* (1976). The board denied Coxe admission to the Mississippi licensing examination because his educational background was judged not to be "primarily psychological in nature." Coxe had received his degree from the University of Southern Mississippi in the department of counseling and guidance. Such departments, despite their name, have for a number of years had graduates who became licensed or certified as psychologists. Some of these departments were authorized by the board of trustees of institutions of higher learning in their state to offer a course of study in counseling psychology. Coxe's challenge to the board was that he was a psychologist in terms of training and professional affiliation and had graduated from a department so authorized. On the basis of the hearings and testimony presented, the court ordered that a license be granted to Coxe. The court noted that the language of the section of the Mississippi law specifying the educational requirements does not narrowly define the kind of educational experiences that are psychological in nature, and the board had not adopted rules to determine whether an educational training program qualified as psychology or not. Without explicit criteria, the court found in favor of the applicant. By ordering that Coxe be licensed and not just admitted to the examination, the court went even further than requested. In other words, the court itself determined that the applicant was competent to practice as a psychologist. The state board of examiners unsuccessfully appealed the decision, and the ruling stands as final.

The case of *Traweek* v. *Alabama Board of Examiners in Psychology* (1976) was similar in that the plaintiff received his doctorate with a major in educational psychology and counseling and guidance. In 1976, having already been licensed in two states but declared ineligible for reciprocity in Alabama, he applied to take the examination and was informed that his preparation in psychology was insufficient to qualify for admission. The board ruled that his transcript did not show sufficient coverage of the basic principles, methods, and procedures of psychology. The plaintiff contended that his major in educational psychology indicated that he had a doctoral degree in psychology. The court made the unexpected ruling that, since the Alabama license is generic and the plaintiff was trained as a specialist in educational psychology, he had not received a doctoral degree in psychology as required by the law. The plaintiff's petition was denied and his later motion to alter, vacate, or amend judgment was ruled against; another appeal has not been filed.

The third case, *Carrol* v. *Florida Board of Examiners* (1976), involved a plaintiff with a master's degree in clinical psychology and a doctoral degree in pupil personnel services. The plaintiff's major field of study was titled "counseling psychology." The hearing officers, citing the rules of the Florida Board of Examiners of Psychology that defined acceptable graduate training, determined that the doctoral degree did not constitute a degree in psychology from a university program maintaining a standard of training comparable to that of universities whose programs are approved by the American Psychological Association (APA) (the criterion used in the Florida rules).

In 1978, Greensfelden, a counseling psychologist in Missouri, appealed the decision of the Missouri Committee of Psychologists not to license her. The committee, following guidelines similar to those of the 1977 Education and Credentialing Conference, had ruled that she did not meet course work requirements in their five required core areas. A state administrative hearing commissioner ruled that, since the actual statute does not mention core areas, the commission exceeded its statutory authority ("Requirements for Licensing Psychologists Are Ruled Invalid," 1979). A final ruling on whether Greenfelden had to be licensed was not available as of this writing. The decision will affect up to 180 other self-identified psychologists in Missouri who have been denied licenses (one of whom, ironically enough, is a former director of the state mental health department).

What the court cases have made clear is that when the applicable statute or rules of procedures for the board do not clearly define what training is acceptable as being psychological in nature, it is difficult to sustain denials. The Missouri case goes further, suggesting that definitions must be contained in the statute itself rather than only in the procedures. For this reason many states have been very quick to adopt the guidelines developed in the 1977 Education and Credentialing Conference (see Chapter Three), which define the administrative features and content required for a program in psychology.

Other court challenges to psychology licensing boards of the past decade involved qualifying for licensing less directly but may be of general interest. Smith (1978) reviews court challenges regarding grandfather regulations, evaluation of candidates (a board's right to set cutoff points for the objective examination and to include controversial examination items), and enforcement of licensing regulations. The most frequently cited case in the last category involved a person from the field of counseling (*State of Ohio* v. *Cook,* Cleveland Municipal Court, 75 CRB 11478, 1975). When the 1972 psychology licensing statute was enacted in Ohio, Cook, trained in counseling and guidance, had a part-time practice in the mental assessment of children. He wrote the Ohio board himself "concerning the nature of his practice to insure that his undertaking would not result in problems with the board. After a month had passed without response from the Ohio board, he wrote again to inquire of the board's position on such matters. A few weeks later he was arrested for practicing psychology without a license, still without having received a directed response from the board. The judge who heard the case handed down a direct verdict in favor of the defendant, and refused to hear even the arguments of the Ohio Board on the matter" (Smith, 1978, p. 496). Smith goes on to say that the failure of the Ohio board to follow its own rules in enforcement matters, that is, its failure to communicate with the defendant prior to his arrest, prompted the court's action.

Qualification Issues

Problems repeatedly encountered by applicants for state licensure or certification will continue to be significant, especially if more states adopt the guidelines of the 1977 Education and Credentialing meeting and the concepts of the proposed National Commission for the Designation of Doctoral Programs in Psychology. Five problems frequently affect applicants, especially those who are not trained in traditional psychology departments. These include the administrative location and format of the training department, the type of course work, the nature of internship, the type of university accreditation, and specialty licensing. The latter four areas are of concern to all candidates for licensing as psychologists, even those from clearly labeled or APA-approved psychology doctoral programs.

Applicants Trained Outside of Psychology Departments. Counseling, school, rehabilitation, developmental, educational, and, increasingly, industrial-organizational psychologists often receive their graduate training outside of psychology departments. Counseling psychologists are the largest group, at least in terms of the number seeking licensing, and their situation is described in detail.

Even from the outset of the profession in the early 1950s, much of the training in counseling psychology has been conducted outside of psychology departments. About half of all members of the APA Division Counseling Psychology received their degrees outside of departments of psychology; well over half of the APA-approved programs in counseling psychology are housed totally or partially outside of psychology departments. Given these facts and the fact that counseling psychology is one of the largest professional specialties within psychology, it is not surprising that a great many issues regarding licensing have occurred in this field.

Recognizing this long-standing diversity of educational backgrounds in several specialties in psychology, state laws originally defined necessary training as being in psychology or "primarily psychological in nature." Of course, this provision encouraged some persons with less than clear (or adequate) credentials to represent themselves as psychologists. Counseling psychologists were especially likely to do so, since they had the most clearly established precedent of qualifying for licensure without receiving degrees from psychology departments. This trend has probably been intensified by the recent tight job market and demographic changes, which have resulted in fewer and fewer positions for people in pupil personnel services, counselor education, and human development and made the still expanding market for service-providing psychologists more attractive.

Recently many states and employers have found that over one-half of their applicants for licensing or psychology positions have received their degrees outside of psychology departments. As mentioned earlier in the section on the national conferences on training and credentialing, a survey of what defined "primarily psychological in nature" showed that the label was a euphemism for "not psychology." Examining boards lacking clear rules of operation were forced to make decisions about the adequacy of various theology degrees, communications arts degrees, as well as the entire spectrum of educational administration and service degrees. Most traditionally trained psychologists could say that the problem would be solved quickly and easily by requiring that the degree be from a psychology department; this position, put forth in the 1976 conference, created the furor that led to the establishment of a blue ribbon panel in the counseling division to address this issue with the American Association of State Psychology Boards (AASPB). Much to the credit of this panel, at the 1977 conference the stipulation was changed to read "the program, wherever administratively housed," which allows a psychology program to be located in any department. However, newly required in that latest statement (see Chapter Three), now adopted by over twenty states, is that the program be labeled a psychology program. As a result, students of programs that have long produced counseling psychologists, developmental psychologists, or industrial-organizational psychologists will no longer be eligible for licensing in many states if the programs are labeled counseling and guidance, human development, or organizational development.

We wish to go on record about our concerns over the sudden adoption of these guidelines and their effect on students who were pursuing doctorates in such programs when the guidelines were first discussed. While the concept was accepted by many nontraditional psychologists at the conferences, the assumption was that the guidelines would be implemented in the same reasonable fashion in which most state laws and graduate school curriculum changes are, that is, in a way such that people in the process of obtaining degrees are not penalized by the changes in the regulations. We believe that students in graduate school in the late 1970s, especially those matriculated before 1978 when these guidelines were first widely distributed, should not be penalized for receiving their degrees from outside of psychology departments if their credentials meet the criteria used before the adoption of the 1977 guidelines.

What must be emphasized is that any person who now receives a degree from or is enrolled in a program that is not somehow labeled as a psychology program will encounter significant difficulties in qualifying for licensing or credentialing as a psychologist. Graduates of and students in programs intended to train psychologists but not so labeled need to work closely with their present faculty and university administration to change the program title as quickly as possible. It should be noted that only the program has to be labeled "psychology," not the department in which the program is housed. Therefore, a counseling psychology program can be part of a counseling or education department, and an industrial-organizational psychology program can be part of a college of business.

The adoption of the 1977 guidelines seems to have increased the cavalierism with which state boards reject an application if the applicant's transcript does not clearly show a degree awarded by a department of psychology. Even persons who have obtained degrees from APA-approved programs not housed in psychology departments have been so rejected. Yet the guidelines unambiguously indicate that APA-approved programs meet the criteria for a graduate to be designated as a psychologist. Programs approved by the APA should have transcripts stamped with an appropriate notation, such as "Degree granted by an APA-approved program." Such notation should preclude the offhand rejection of transcripts simply because they lack the word *psychology* in the course descriptions.

Course Work. For applicants whose degrees are from outside of psychology departments, licensing boards usually conduct a review of the course work first. In many nontraditional programs, all courses may be labeled "education" or "business" rather than "psychology," even though the syllabi and texts may be identical to those for courses taught in psychology departments and the courses even taught by credentialed psychologists. The same leeway in regulations that gave well-trained persons the option for this review allowed people not trained in psychology the same option. Prospective licensees should note that as long as course equivalence is considered (and this provision may well disappear if a national designation system for psychology programs is implemented), the three factors that usually receive close attention are the content of the course (as evidenced by the syllabus), the text used in the course, and the qualifications of the instructor. A course in human development, for example, could be essentially identical to a course in developmental psychology or child psychology; on the other hand, such a course could deal strictly with a biological, sociological, or educational perspective that would not be appropriate for a psychology course.

Prospective licensees in a degree program outside of a department of psychology who can take psychology courses as part of their curricula provide much clearer evidence that their education is primarily psychological. Some state boards ask the applicant to get a psychology department member to specify that the course content is equivalent to a course offered in the psychology department. This is not a role that psychology faculty welcome or usually accept willingly, but it is one that can be explored.

For licensure applicants from any program, within or outside of a psychology department, the guidelines proposed in 1977 have added a new dimension to the course work requirements. Those standards (see Chapter Three) specify that the student must demonstrate competence (through course work or in other ways) in four areas in psychology: biological bases of behavior, cognitive-affective bases, social bases, and individual differences. Clearly, students currently working toward degrees in any program, including those labeled as psychology programs and APA-approved programs, should make sure that they have evidence of assessment, at the graduate level, of their competence in those four areas. Whether states that have adopted the guidelines are making them requirements for all students, regardless of whether the students are from approved or clearly labeled psychology programs, is yet unclear. Students not from APA-approved programs must consider course work or other evidence of competence in these four areas as essential, and wherever possible, such courses should be completed under the instruction of clearly labeled psychology faculty.

Supervised Experience. Many psychologists have had problems meeting supervised experience requirements for state and federal civil service agencies and for the National Register of Health Service Providers in Psychology (see Chapter Eight), even though these psychologists believed they had suitable predoctoral internships and postdegree experience. First consideration is given to predoctoral internships; counseling psychologists seem to have had the most difficulties in meeting standards in this area. Specialties in psychology other than clinical, counseling, and school psychology usually do not have internships. For nearly twenty years clinical psychology has had rather specific and strong statements regarding the nature of an internship. During the 1960s, even membership in the APA Division of Clinical Psychology required the completion of such an internship. Counseling psychology has never taken as firm a stance, and indeed, up until the 1970s, several APA-approved counseling psychology programs did not require an internship. Those internships that have been required typically (1) last less than twelve months, because of the frequency of counseling psychologists' internships in academic settings (where an academic year lasts nine or ten months); (2) are often half-time or less rather than full-time, cumulating credit towards the required nine-, ten-, or twelve-month assignment; (3) are often completed in an organization that may not be considered as a health-service-providing agency, such as a marriage counseling agency or career development center; and (4) are sometimes not supervised by a psychologist but rather by a social worker or guidance counselor.

Each of these four factors directly affects the evaluation of the internship by credentialing agencies. The clinical psychology standard has generally been a twelve-month, full-time placement in a single institution under the supervision of a clearly identified psychologist. The school psychology internship, while usually lasting only for an academic year, has usually been at least half-time or greater, clearly supervised by a psychologist, and in an unambiguously psychological service. The recently approved criteria for APA accreditation (see Chapter Seven for details) specify that the internship must last at least an academic year for counseling and school psychologists and a calendar year for clinical psychologists and be completed in no less than half-time placements for two years. Qualified psychologists must supervise. Academic credit is rarely given for the internship experience (though it may be for the prerequisite practica). Prospective licensees should consider these standards when arranging for their internships, since any deviations from them may lead to an experience that will not meet the supervised experience requirement. Such an applicant would then have to arrange for a new placement to accumulate the specified number of hours of such supervised experience.

Another aspect of the internship is the mode and amount of supervision provided. In all fields of psychology, considering participation in case conferences, staff meetings, and the like as supervision and accepting as little as one hour per week of individual supervision have been common. Revised criteria for the approval of internships (see Chapter Seven) specify intensive individual supervision at least two hours per week, and more time is desirable. Again, this standard should be observed when arranging internships.

Many agencies, such as state civil service commissions and the Veterans Administration, require 1,900 or 2,000 hours of internship experience to qualify for psychologist positions. Therefore, students in programs that require only a nine- or ten-month internship will need to arrange for additional placement or additional hours on their initial internship. A student's program director or supervisor must usually testify to the number of supervised hours completed.

Another internship issue that emerged in 1978 is now being referred to appropriate bodies in the APA for action in 1980—the increasing frequency with which employment positions require that the candidate have an APA-approved internship as well as a degree from an APA-approved program.

Several approved programs have taken issue with what appears to be a redundancy of requirements. APA approval of a training program requires proper monitoring and reporting of students interning in other than APA-approved agencies and justification of such placement. In other words, directors of approved training programs believe that all their graduates hold the equivalent of APA-approved internships; this has been an implicit understanding for the past few decades. If this understanding no longer exists, then several effective but often small and sometimes "captive" internship settings that are not eligible for independent accreditation would no longer be suitable placements despite adequate training.

This issue is coming before the Committee on Accreditation of the APA in 1980; readers who have not yet completed an internship should monitor this issue carefully before choosing a placement. (Captive settings refer to agencies that have an exclusive agreement with a training program to train students only from that program.)

State Versus Regional Accreditation. Many professionals are unaware that many schools and universities are chartered for operation by state boards of education but do not have and could not qualify for regional accreditation. Please note that the 1977 Education and Credentialing Conference as well as the standards for accreditation by the APA and the criteria for the National Register (see Chapters Seven and Eight, respectively) require regional accreditation of a school. See Chapter Seven for a description of the recognized regional accreditation associations. In short, a degree from a school legitimately authorized to operate in a given state but not approved by one of the regional accreditation bodies may leave one uncontestably ineligible for a position or credentialing as a psychologist.

Specialty Licensing. At the present time, there is considerable discussion within the psychology community as to whether generic licensing and credentialing should be deemphasized in favor of specialized licensing, for example, licensing in counseling psychology, clinical psychology, industrial-organizational psychology, school psychology, and the like. Industrial-organizational psychologists especially have been increasingly concerned that laws and regulations about licensing are being written that deal primarily with health service delivery and third-party payments from insurance policies, domains unrelated to the practice of industrial-organizational psychology. However, licensing does affect this group, since they are providing services for a fee and must be licensed to operate in many states. Specialty credentialing could, of course, make the necessary exceptions desired by industrial-organizational psychologists.

The major problem that specialty credentialing presents to the health-service-providing fields (such as clinical, counseling, community, and school psychology) is that it would probably limit what is at present a fairly high degree of interchangeability of many functions. Unless specialty regulations are written broadly, it could be difficult for clinical psychologists to operate in school or counseling center settings, or for counseling psychologists to operate in psychiatric hospital settings or community mental health centers. If the specialty standards were written broadly enough to avoid this problem, how could these specialties then be differentiated?

If specialty licensing is implemented, some psychology specialties that have long served in particular settings may be prohibited from continuing to do so. This phenomenon has occurred in Virginia, which in 1976 established a statute that licensed clinical psychologists separately from generic psychologists. Although both types of psychologists can maintain private practices, only licensed clinical psychologists can receive third-party payment from insurance companies. Consequently, a number of community mental health centers, which rely significantly on third-party payments, have refused to hire counseling psychologists and community psychologists, even though such persons had traditionally been trained by and employed by their staffs. Moreover, counseling psychologists examined under the generic psychology act have been informed that they may not practice skills for which they have received training if the skills are classified as part of clinical psychology (J. W. McIntire, personal communication, 1979).

Other states have considered laws similar to Virginia's. Nebraska provides specialty certification for clinical psychology that is appended to the generic license; Texas presently authorizes specialty certification for clinical, school, counseling, and industrial-organizational psychology and is under legislative mandate to consider establishing specialty licensing for the first three; California provides separate licensure for educational psychologists; and Ohio, Virginia, and Wisconsin grant separate licenses for school psychology. Each of these specialty designations involves training requirements and practice limitations in comparison with the generic license.

Because of the large number of clinical psychologists and their greater representation on most licensing boards, school, counseling, community, and industrial-organizational psychologists often perceive themselves as disadvantaged by specialty licenses or certifications. The concept of specialties is also expanding to include biofeedback psychologists, psychoanalysts, behavioral psychologists, and the like. Obviously members of any specialty outside of traditional clinical psychology should carefully monitor specialty legislation to insure that training and practice requirements are fair.

Training for Psychologists Wishing to Change Their Specialty

A policy developed primarily for experimental psychologists has been increasingly employed by psychologists having difficulty in achieving licensable credentials, especially specialty credentials. In the past few years, a number of persons originally trained in areas such as experimental and social psychology have sought to establish credentials as clinical or counseling psychologists. In 1976, recognizing the issues involved in such changes and responding to some reports of persons adopting new professional titles after taking only a postdoctoral internship (or less), the APA Council of Representatives adopted a policy on training for psychologists wishing to change their specialty. This document is now being recognized for health-service-providing psychologists who wish to establish credentials of another kind, for example, for a school psychologist to become recognized as a counseling psychologist, or a counseling psychologist to become recognized as a clinical psychologist. According to this document, the steps that are necessary for psychologists to change their specialty are as follows:

> Psychologists seeking to change their specialty should take training in a program of the highest quality, and, where appropriate, exemplified by the doctoral training programs and internships accredited by the APA: with respect to subject matter and professional skills, *psychologists taking such training must meet all requirements of doctoral training in the new psychological specialty, being given due credit for relevant course work or requirements* they have previously satisfied; it must be stressed, however, that merely taking an internship or acquiring experience in a practicum setting is not, for example, considered adequate preparation for becoming a clinical, counseling, or school psychologist when prior training had not been in the relevant area; upon fulfillment of all formal requirements of such training programs, the students *should be awarded a certificate* indicating the successful completion of preparation in the particular specialty, thus according them due recognition

for their additional education and experience [American Psychological Association, Council of Representatives, 1976].

Grandparenting

Grandfather (now grandparent) clauses were included in most states' statutes so that licenses could be granted, sometimes without examination, to individuals engaged in psychological practice at the time that the law was enacted. Because most laws were enacted a number of years ago, grandparent clauses have now expired in every state and province. Such clauses enabled many persons without doctoral degrees or with doctoral degrees in other fields who established practice as a psychologist to continue their practices.

Such clauses may reenter the licensing picture for two reasons. First, the effects of sunset laws and other challenges to the concepts of licensing, as reviewed in preceding chapters, may result in totally new laws. If the new laws are radically different from the previous laws, some grandparent clauses may be included. Second, some states are eliminating exemptions from licensing for people employed in service settings. Many laws were primarily meant to apply to people who were providing services for a fee, and they exempted all persons employed by municipal, state, or federal institutions. Consistent with the APA standards for service providers (see Chapter Seven), many of these exemptions are now being withdrawn. As this occurs, some states are considering grandparent clauses that allow persons satisfactorily employed at the time that the clause takes effect to retain their positions. The Veterans Administration has included such a stipulation in a recent proposal to require licensing of all psychologists. In other words, persons presently and satisfactorily employed by the Veterans Administration but not licensed and due to their credentials unable to achieve licensing will still retain their employment.

All psychologists need to be aware of changes in employment practices of major institutions and proposed changes by state licensing agencies; the profession must ensure that any changes include appropriate grandparent clauses.

Examination for Professional Practice in Psychology

The EPPP was developed at the request of the AASPB. The first form was administered in 1964 and has since been revised seven times. As of early 1979, every state except Arizona has used or soon plans to use the EPPP.

> Test development . . . has always leaned heavily upon the voluntary participation of qualified psychologists throughout the APA. Items are contributed by psychologists recognized in their specialty areas. To date, nearly 300 psychologists have contributed items. These are edited by members of the examination committee and staff members of PES [Professional Examination Service; address in appendix]. Each item selected is then scrutinized by at least three reviewers known for their expertise in representing the leadership and rank and file of American psychology. . . . For Form 5, 97% of the items showed a discrimination index significant at the .01 level. The corrected split half reliability is .906 [Carlson, 1978, p. 491].

For further information on the psychometric aspects of the examination, see Terris (1973). Terris also explains the use of the tests by various boards: "Boards set their own cutoff points, which differ from state to state; most commonly, this written test is the only regularly administered examination for all candidates for licensure; boards that administer other examinations usually give essay or oral examinations; generally speaking, no formal weights are assigned to any particular examination pattern" (p. 389). The items for recent forms of the exam through early 1980 were drawn from categories similar to those shown in Table 4.

Both psychologists and consumer representatives have questioned the validity of the examination (see Carsten, 1978). In response, the Executive Committee of the AASPB has recommended that the examination be expanded to 300 items to strengthen the validity studies. The examination fee (which state boards must pay for each examinee) was increased in 1978 to $60 in order to generate, over the following three years,

Table 4. Categories for Items in the 1978 Examination for
Professional Practice in Psychology

Background
    History, theory, and systems
    Physiological psychology and comparative psychology
    Sensation and perception
    Learning
    Cognition
    Motivation
    Developmental psychology
    Personality
    Social psychology

Methodology
    Research design and interpretation
    Statistics
    Test construction and interpretation
    Evaluation, reliability, and validation processes

Professional Conduct, Affairs, Ethics, and Accountability
    Professional conduct and ethics
    Knowledge of professional affairs

Intervention and Other Applications
    Behavior disorders, deviance, and dysfunction
    Diagnosis and evaluation
    Therapy and other intervention
    Community psychology and mental health
    Behavior modification
    Management consulting, industrial and human engineering
    Counseling and guidance
    Communications, systems and analysis
    Education and school

Source: Adapted from "Professional Examination Service Issues and Activities,"
1978, p. 11.

$150,000 to $200,000 for validation research. However, many
questions remain to be answered.

What is actually being measured by the EPPP? How
well does the content of the examination, both in general
areas and individual items, relate to the domain of tasks
and activities of today's psychologist at the point of
entry into the profession? . . . Are the . . . specialty areas
of practice adequately reflected, both quantitatively and
qualitatively? Is every eligible candidate, regardless of
theoretical or career orientation, provided with an equal
opportunity to display a score performance reflective of

minimally required competence? How can the examination content be improved to better serve its stated purpose?

How does performance on the EPPP correlate with performance on other measures which presumably relate to, or predict, success in psychology?

Are persons who score at varying levels on the EPPP characterized or typified by any identifiable characteristics, such as personal data, biographical information, education history, specialization in education or career, employment history or status, subjective or other data obtained and rated by boards, incidence or type of complaints lodged against them ["National Written Examination," 1978, p. 13].

By late 1979, a blue ribbon panel of psychologists, representing five areas of professional practice, had defined a list of roles and knowledges necessary for professional practice. The major categories in these lots included techniques for appraising and assessing clients and patients, uses of techniques in research, elements in training and supervision, the design, implementation, and assessment of interventions, and professional and ethical issues. Six to fourteen specific content areas have been outlined for each of these domains. At present, a broad sampling of professional psychologists is being asked to help determine those aspects of professional practice that can be accurately measured on an objective multiple-choice examination. The revised package will then be rated by a large sample of both experienced and newly licensed professional psychologists in order to develop a new test.

In the past, validation studies were usually unsystematic and limited to an analysis of relationships between the demographic, educational, and professional characteristics of examinees and their scores. "Ph.D. holders, for example, have scored significantly higher than other degree groups. APA Fellows and Members have performed better than Associate Members and non-Members. Even at the undergraduate level, performance of a group of psychology honor society students showed positive relationships to the number of psychology courses taken and to grade point averages. Among career psychologists, those trained in clinical and industrial and social specialties earned significantly higher scores than those trained in experimental, counseling and educational psychology" ("National Written Examination," 1978, p. 11). Hays and Schreiner (1977) compared Ph.D. and Ed.D. examinees in Texas in 1975 and found that the Ph.D.'s were significantly more likely to attain the state's passing standard (minus one-half deviation below the national mean). Of the Ph.D. examinees, 113 passed and 15 failed; of the Ed.D. examinees, 21 passed and 11 failed.

The AASPB administers the examination on set dates each year and provides an interstate reporting service for candidates who wish to have their scores reported to several states.

It is important to note that the Professional Examination Service is *not* involved in the preparatory review programs and workshops advertised for the national psychology examination. These programs have been developed by independent psychologists and other persons aware of the fact that many persons fail this examination and therefore become ineligible for licensing. As more and more states use this examination, more and more of these programs have been developed along with study manuals and workshops.

Like most examination preparation programs, there is no clear evidence that these programs are more effective in improving one's scores than self-study of the content areas listed in Table 4. The workshops are probably more helpful for persons with a limited background in psychology. Many persons who have had broad-based training in their doctoral work in psychology have found that an intensive review of an introductory psychology text helps them to obtain a passing grade on the national examination.

5

Licensing
of Counselors

The history of licensing counselors is relatively brief compared
to that of licensing psychologists. Personnel and guidance counseling was first legally recognized as a profession separate from
psychology in 1972 (*Weldon* v. *Board of Psychologist Examiners,* 1972). In this case, Weldon, a counselor engaged in private practice, argued that he was exempt from the state psychology licensure laws because guidance and counseling were
fields separate from psychology. The Virginia State Board of
Psychologist Examiners disagreed and secured a court order
restraining Weldon from practicing. Weldon appealed, where-
upon the court "disagreed with the Virginia State Board of
Psychologist Examiners in holding that appellant is practicing
psychology, thus requiring him to be licensed under the laws of
the state of Virginia." The court held that "the profession of
personnel and guidance counseling is a separate profession and
should be so recognized." However, "this profession does utilize
the tools of the psychologist as [do] many other professions,
therefore it would be necessary for him [Weldon] to be licensed

79

under existing laws" (Van Hoose and Kottler, 1977, p. 122). The decision thus seemed contradictory. The judge noted, however, that he felt bound by the Virginia statute that "appears to say" that if a counselor uses the tools of psychology, in the absence of a regulatory body governing guidance and personnel counseling, a counselor in private practice is subject to the laws governing the practice of psychology.

Prompted by the Weldon case, Virginia became the first state to enact legislation for counselors. In 1975 the following statutes were enacted: "Guidance and personnel counseling means the application of those principles of guidance and personnel functions which focus upon the developmental process of a person in relation to educational and social progress, and occupational and career goals." At the request of the Virginia Personnel and Guidance Association, the 1976 Virginia general assembly amended this statute with the following definition: "Professional counselor shall mean a person trained in counseling and guidance services with emphasis on individual and group counseling designed to assist individuals in achieving more effective personal, social, educational and career development and adjustment."

This law was the first to license counselors in private practice. (From 1974 to 1979, six states also licensed marriage and family therapists, as listed later in this chapter.) In 1979, licensing for counselors was approved in three additional states: Arkansas, Alabama, and New Hampshire. New Hampshire licenses only master's-level rehabilitation counselors, whereas the other two states instituted generic licensing for master's-level counselors. In several other states, licensing legislation for counseling has passed at least one legislative house between 1975 and 1979. From 1976 to 1979, the number of states introducing legislation for counselors rose from six to twenty-four. As of early 1979, forty-one states had counselor licensing committees; thirty-one had already adopted supportive position statements ("Pre-legislative Summary Spotlighted at Meeting," 1979). Given the recent successful attempts at licensure and the sustained efforts by counselors to promote legislation and to work cooperatively with other groups such as social workers

("Counselors to Join Social Workers," 1979), the number of states that license counselors is likely to increase.

Counselors have argued that counselor licensure laws have emerged because psychology licensing laws have (1) denied credentialing to persons who because of their training believe they are qualified to provide mental health services and (2) restricted the practices of these persons. Counselors have filed legal grievances against psychology boards in at least twenty states (*Licensure Committee Action Packet,* 1979).

The number of professional persons involved in these concerns is already in the thousands and continues to grow. A recent survey by the American Personnel and Guidance Association (APGA) ("Demographic Study Shows APGA Status," 1979) shows that over 2,000 member counselors were involved in private practice or primarily serving in a private counseling setting. Nearly 4,000 other counselors were engaged in part-time private practice or employed at private counseling centers. Nearly 16,000 members indicated that their primary professional identification was as a counselor rather than as a counselor educator, student personnel worker, measurement specialist, or the like. The American Mental Health Counselors Association asserts that nearly 100,000 mental health counselors provide 57 percent of all mental health services ("AMHCA Seeks Amendment to Health Bill," 1980).

Carroll, Halligan, and Griggs (1977) provide data on the effects of psychology licensing on counselors. In a survey of the 4,285 members of the Association of Counselor Educators and Supervisors, which had a 40 percent response rate, 97 of the 388 respondents who applied for a psychology licensing examination were declared ineligible. Almost two-thirds of the refusals came from the states of Alabama, California, Colorado, Florida, Georgia, Louisiana, Mississippi, New York, Texas, and Virginia. Seventy counselors reported that they had been denied employment in a clinic or agency because of Medicare or other insurance policies, which would not make payments for services offered by unlicensed professional counselors. Extrapolation suggests that some 170 counselors were thus denied employment for which they were trained. Of all the respondents, 45.4

percent believed that the master's was the lowest acceptable degree for being licensed for private practice; 41.6 percent that believed the doctorate was necessary; and 13 percent gave other educational qualifications, ranging from a bachelor's degree with demonstrated experience to two years of clinical practice in an accredited agency.

Sweeney and Sturdevant (1974) identify the kind of psychology legislation that significantly affects counselors. They note that laws that are essentially certification laws have little effect on counselor educators or supervisors. However, counselors must carefully attend to such laws as the 1972 Ohio law, which limits who can conduct certain kinds of services and practices. Many positions that graduates of counselor education programs often enter, for example, positions in various community mental health centers and university counseling centers, are subject to state laws on licensing for psychologists. Teaching and supervising counseling courses, even outside of psychology departments, also seem to come under the purview of the Ohio law. The Cook case (see Chapter Four) illustrates the difficulties that counselors face who are not licensed as psychologists—a license for which most counselors are declared ineligible.

Another factor that is increasing the pressure for licensing in counseling is qualifying for third-party payments. Psychologists have had a long, difficult struggle to obtain direct reimbursement in several states; in other states, psychologists as well as most other professionals must be supervised by a psychiatrist in order to be eligible for reimbursement. Asher (1979) expressed concerns about the survival of the counselor's profession when she noted that the President's Commission on Mental Health proposed that counselors and other noncore professionals be reimbursed for services only if the services are provided under the direct clinical supervision of a physician, psychologist, social worker, or nurse. Asher states that the failure of the commission to recognize master's-level counselors as the equals of master's-level social workers and nurses represents a continuation of the status quo.

In the past several years the APGA and the American Association for Marriage and Family Therapy (AAMFT) have increased their efforts to develop state licensing and certification. In the next two sections the activities of each organization pertaining to counselor licensing are reviewed. The somewhat surprising emergence of licensing of rehabilitation counselors in New Hampshire in 1979 is also mentioned.

Licensing Activities of the APGA

In 1975, the senate of the APGA adopted "a position in favor of vigorous, responsible action to establish the provisions for the licensure of professional counselors in the various states. A licensure commission was formed at that time with three tasks: 1) to collect and disseminate information about licensure development at the state and national level, 2) to assist members in state groups to resolve licensure problems at the legislative, professional, or examining board level, 3) to provide national leadership on counselor licensure needs by seeking active relationships with other professional organizations, state and local government agencies, and state legislative bodies" (Cottingham and Warner, 1978). Cottingham and Warner also examine the internal and external pressures that brought about the creation of the commission, citing many of the same factors noted in this chapter's introduction. The commission has undertaken a number of projects, the most obvious of which is the publication of an annually updated "action packet" (*Licensure Committee Action Packet,* 1979). The contents of this packet are reviewed later in this chapter.

Additionally, the commission has developed a national register of counselors, a third-party payment bill, a national licensure network, regional and state workshops, and procedures for handling licensing complaints. It has also maintained dialogues with such related groups as the National Association of Social Workers, the American Psychological Association, the AAMFT, the Federal Trade Commission, and the Veterans Administration.

Forster (1978) has reviewed the broad support for additional credentialing that developed after the establishment of the commission in 1975. Not only has the APGA provided leadership in the development of the licensure commission, but various member organizations of APGA have also vigorously participated in various licensing activities in recent years. The Association of Counselor Educators and Supervisors, the American School Counselors Association, and the American College Personnel Association have all developed licensure task forces or comparable groups.

In his summary of the commission's accomplishments of the past few years, Forster (1978, p. 595) notes:

> Suddenly, counselors are trying to convince judges and legislatures that counseling is, in fact, separate and different from psychology. This new necessity seems to be doing more to clarify the identity of the profession than have years of conferences and commissions devoted to identifying counselor roles and functions. . . . I have identified three related factors for distinguishing between counseling and psychology: the practitioner's education level, the emphasis on psychopathology, and the focus of the method. Although many would agree with Patterson (1974), that these distinctions are artificial and nearly impossible to make, it appears as if we have in fact started to distinguish between counseling and psychology along these dimensions.

Licensure Committee Action Packet. The *Licensure Committee Action Packet* (1979) is the most thorough set of preparatory materials that any professional organization of counselors or psychologists has made available to its members. This pack, in addition to describing many of the developments and accomplishments of the APGA licensure commission, provides (1) detailed outlines of reasons for counselor licensure; (2) discussions of professional and economic issues in licensure; (3) detailed responses to questions that legislators frequently ask about licensure (see Chapter Six); (4) outlines for licensure workshops; and (5) an outline, which is basically an organizational manual, for legislative action. This final outline gives preliminary steps to obtaining legislative action, essential background information, procedures for developing support within the profession, information on preparing a draft bill, and information on how to work with legislators to increase the likelihood of the legislature and governor approving a counselor licensure bill.

A section in the packet also discusses how counselors might try to change psychology licensing laws rather than obtain counselor licensure. "Counselors and other helping professions can join forces and work for legislation authorizing the formation of broad behavior science boards or seek a revision of current restrictive psychology licensure laws and board policies. . . . Another avenue might be consultation with legislative committees charged with holding hearings to implement sunset legislation, dealing with the accountability of state occupational boards" (*Licensure Committee Action Packet,* p. 17). The packet text acknowledges that the impetus for counselor licensure has come from the exclusion of counselors by psychologists. The text also mentions that if collaboration with other helping professions cannot be easily arranged, some increased willingness for cooperation might be stimulated by threats to publicize counselors' accomplishments at hearings to implement sunset legislation. While this suggestion is offensive to many because it promotes the negative effects of sunset legislation, many people feel greatly deprived because they have been excluded from the careers for which they were trained by overly prescriptive psychology licensing laws.

The packet also provides suggested legislative language for a counselor licensure law (see below) as well as copies of the successful Virginia and Alabama laws and the 1978 North Carolina bill, which was not passed. With a network of representatives from almost every state heading up a licensure committee, counselors have, in addition to this written material, ready access to many other knowledgeable and experienced counselors working on licensure. The packet may be purchased from the APGA (address in appendix); readers are urged to reproduce any and all material in the packet.

Suggested Legislative Language for Counseling Licensure Laws. The suggested legislative language and the supporting rationale for each section take up over 500 lines of print in the

Licensure Committee Action Packet (1979). The major proposals plus those definitions and stipulations that are most controversial among the affected professions or among legislatures
are listed later in this chapter. Readers wishing full details
should consult the *Licensure Committee Action Packet.*

The suggested definition of a licensed counselor is as follows: "Licensed professional counselor means and is restricted
to any person who holds himself/herself out to the public by
any title or description of services incorporating the words
'licensed professional counselor'; and who offers to render professional counseling services to individuals, groups, organizations, corporations, institutions, government agencies or the
general public for a fee, monetary or otherwise, implying that
s/he is licensed and trained, experienced or expert in counseling,
and who holds a current, valid license to practice counseling"
(*Licensure Committee Action Packet,* 1979, p. 23).

The suggested qualifications for applicants include that
the applicant be at least nineteen years of age, be a citizen of
the United States or intend to become one, be of good moral
character, and not have violated any provisions of the licensure
act.

With regard to education, it is proposed that "the applicant [have] . . . a master's degree from a regionally accredited
institution of higher education, which is primarily counseling in
content and which meets the academic and training content
standards established by the board, or the substantial equivalent
in both subject matter and extent of training. The board shall
use the standards of appropriate counseling associations as a
guide in establishing the standards for counselor licensure (that
is, APGA Standards for the Preparation of Counselors and
Other Personnel Services Specialists)" (*Licensure Committee
Action Packet,* p. 24).

Regarding experience, "the applicant [should have] . . .
three years of supervised full-time experience in professional
counseling acceptable to the board, one year of which may be
obtained prior to the granting of the master's degree. An applicant may subtract one year of the required professional experience for every 30 graduate semester hours obtained beyond the

master's degree, provided such hours are clearly related to the field of professional counseling and are acceptable to the board. However, in no case may the applicant have less than one year of the required professional experience" (*Licensure Committee Action Packet,* 1979, p. 24). Regarding examination for licensure, it is recommended that "the applicant [demonstrate] . . . professional competence in specialty areas by passing an examination, written and/or oral and/or performance as the board will prescribe" (p. 24).

Other sections of the bill deal with statement of policy, enabling clauses, establishment of a professional counselor licensing board, and defining supervised experience, continuing education, privileged communication, and ethical violations. The counselor licensing board is advised to adopt a code of ethics appropriate for a professional counseling association.

Restricted employment and specialty designation clauses are suggested, in contrast to traditional psychology licensing laws. The restricted employment clause is inserted for those "concerned groups of persons in drug, alcohol, rehabilitation, and employment settings who may perceive licensure legislation as a means of displacing them from jobs that they now hold" (*Licensure Committee Action Packet,* p. 27). The language of the proposed clause attempts to distinguish between those persons licensed to practice counseling and those who are simply registered or certified through nonstatutory recognition programs as described in Chapter Eight in this book. Obviously, such a section is intended to preclude the kind of divisiveness that psychology laws have so often created for recognized specialists, such as master's-level school psychologists.

Specialty designation language is recommended when desirable (although "when desirable" is not further specified) for "certifying or licensing persons of specialty competence for areas of practice in the field of counseling. . . . This recommendation is based upon the belief that there are areas of special competence in counseling which require more intensive or special training, experience, and evidence of expertise, than generalized training can permit" (*Licensure Committee Action Packet,* 1979, p. 27a). This section acknowledges that two types of counselors are already seeking specialty credentialing, marriage and family counselors and rehabilitation counselors. This clause should preclude fighting between these counselors by legitimizing specialty designations.

Also proposed is a limited license for suitably trained but not yet sufficiently experienced counselors; the limited license would require that the person only practice with direct supervision.

Specific exceptions are made for the clergy for those "activities that are in the scope of the performance of their regular or specialized ministerial duties" (*Licensure Committee Action Packet,* 1979, p. 27b).

To foster harmonious interprofessional relations, a provision for licensing without examination is recommended. "Persons who, in the judgment of the board, do not meet the appropriate criteria of this act may be granted a limited license for a period not to exceed five years during which time the person must qualify themselves" (*Licensure Committee Action Packet,* 1979, p. 27d). This stipulation is a limited form of grandparenting that assures legislators that passage of the bill would not immediately deny a person his or her right to continue to earn a living in which they have been gainfully employed before the enactment of the legislation. Given the limited educational and experiential qualifications for counselor licensure, the five-year time period allows any person ample time to comply with the law.

A final, unique feature of the proposed licensing language is the inclusion of a professional disclosure statement: "No licensed or certified counselor and no person or agency that employs a licensed certified counselor shall charge any client a fee for counseling services, unless, prior to performance of the service, the counselor furnishes the client with a copy of a professional disclosure statement" (*Licensure Committee Action Packet,* 1979, p. 28). This statement is in accord with the intent of some alternatives to licensing (see Chapter Two) and the Standards for Providers of Psychological Services; however, this statement gives far more weight to the procedure than do the present standards in psychology.

Licensing Activities of the AAMFT

The AAMFT, founded in 1942, has been very active in the past few years in promoting licensing as well as in developing definitions and qualifications for membership standards, a code of professional ethics, standards for public information advertising and accreditation policies, and procedures for training programs in marriage and family therapy. The association reached a new milestone in 1978 when its Committee on Accreditation was formally recognized as a national accrediting organization for the professional field of marriage and family counseling by the U.S. Department of Health, Education, and Welfare (HEW). This action marked the first time that the federal government has officially acknowledged the existence of marriage and family counseling as a distinct profession. (The accreditation policies and procedures are described in Chapter Seven).

The activities of the AAMFT have directly contributed to the licensure of marriage and family therapists in seven states: California, Georgia, Michigan, New Jersey, Nevada, North Carolina, and Utah. The AAMFT has prepared model law in two forms, one to be used for licensing acts and one for certification acts. A certification law requires that those persons desiring to use the title "marital and family therapist" or to advertise that they perform marital and family therapy must be certified by the state. The licensing law, in addition to requiring a license for those activities for which certification is required, requires anyone who "practices" marital and family therapy to obtain a license.

The licensing law is summarized here; the certification act is essentially the same except for the differences noted earlier. While the model licensing law has thirty-one detailed sections, of most significance to counselors and psychologists are the sections on definitions; prohibited acts; exemptions; grandparenting; and educational, experience, and examination requirements. These sections are quoted or summarized below. Detailed information on all sections may be obtained by requesting the state licensing and certification model legislation from the AAMFT (address in appendix).

The practice of marital and family therapy in the model licensing act is defined as

the rendering of professional marital and family therapy or counseling services to individuals, family groups and marital pairs, singly or in groups whether such services are offered directly to the general public or through organizations, either public or private, for a fee, monetary or otherwise. "Marital and family therapy" is a specialized field of therapy which centers largely upon the family relationship and the relationship between husband and wife. It also includes premarital therapy, predivorce and postdivorce therapy and family therapy. "Marital and family therapy" consists of the application of principles, methods and techniques of therapy, and therapeutic techniques for the purpose of resolving emotional conflict, modifying perception and behavior, altering old attitudes and establishing new ones in the area of marriage and family life [American Association for Marriage and Family Therapy, 1979a, pp. 9-10].

The suggested prohibited acts stipulation states: "No person who is not licensed under this Act shall (a) advertise the performance of marital and family therapy or counseling service by him, (b) use a title or description such as 'marital or marriage therapist, counselor, advisor or consultant,' 'Marriage or marriage and family therapist, counselor, advisor, or consultant,' or any other name, style or description denoting that the person is a marital and family therapist, or (c) practice marital and family therapy or counseling" (American Association for Marriage and Family Therapy, 1979a, p. 10).

Proposed exemptions are as follows:

A person shall be exempt from requirements of this Act (1) if the person is practicing marital and family therapy as part of his duties as an employee of (a) a recognized academic institution, or a federal, state, county or local governmental institution or agency while performing those duties for which he was employed by such an institution, agency or facility; (b) an organization which is nonprofit and which is determined by the Board to meet community needs while performing those duties for which he was employed by such an agency; or (2) if the person is a student of therapy, a marital and family therapy intern or person preparing for the practice of marital and family therapy under qualified supervision in a training institution or facility or supervisory arrangement recognized and approved by the Board, provided he is designated by such titles as "marital therapy intern," "family therapy intern," or others, clearly indicating such training status; or (3) if the person has been issued a temporary permit by the Board to engage in the activities for which licensure is required [American Association for Marriage and Family Therapy, 1979a, pp. 10-11].

The AAMFT model legislation contains minimum education and experience qualifications for licensure applications. These include holding a master's degree in marital and family therapy or counseling from a recognized education institution, or having a terminal degree in an allied mental health profession accompanied by a transcript indicating that the degree was equivalent to a course of study for a master's degree in marital and family therapy. Candidates must have successfully completed two calendar years of post-master's work in the practice of marital and family therapy, with ongoing supervision consistent with the standards of the board. Qualified candidates must pass a written and/or oral examination that includes questions from such theoretical and applied fields as "the Board deems most suitable to test an applicant's knowledge and competence to engage in the practice of marital and family therapy" (American Association for Marriage and Family Therapy, 1979a, pp. 14-15).

The recommended grandparent clause recognizes already licensed psychologists and other marital counselors if they hold:

a minimum of a master's degree from an accredited institution so recognized at the time of granting such degree in marital and family therapy or counseling, family life education, psychology, social work, or a clearly comparable field emphasizing marital and family therapy or counseling, or shall be a clergyman, or physician whose transcripts establish that he has completed an appropriate course of study in a closely allied field, . . . at least three years in the practice of therapy for counseling of a character approved by the Board, subsequent to the granting of a degree described [earlier], . . . two years of which experience must have been in marital and family therapy; or is already licensed . . . in this state in an allied mental health profession as defined by this Act and satisfies the educational requirements for licensure as a marital and family therapist [American Association for Marriage and Family Therapy, 1979a, pp. 13-14].

Rehabilitation Counselor Licensure

Of some surprise even to the counseling profession itself was the licensing in 1979 of rehabilitation counselors in New Hampshire. The law resulted from the efforts of the National Rehabilitation Counseling Association, a division of the National Rehabilitation Association. Master's-level counselors have long been concerned with their exclusion by psychology licensing in New Hampshire; rehabilitation counselors readily developed a licensure bill based on the national certification program that rehabilitation counselors have had in operation for the past six years (see Chapter Eight).

The relatively quick success of this licensure action elicited mixed responses even from rehabilitation counselors, some of whom had been supporting legislation for the broader field of counseling ("New Hampshire Rehabilitation Counselors Gain Licensure," 1979). Richard Hardy, licensure chair of the APGA division of the American Rehabilitation Counseling Association, stated, "I am concerned about the splintering out of rehabilitation counselors as a separate profession. It may cause the licensing efforts of other counselors to lose strength. I'm concerned that other counselors will be left out. We shouldn't follow the route of psychologists, with all the splintering out that has gone on in that profession" (p. 9). The same article reports a survey showing that 86 percent of the rehabilitation counselors surveyed favor some type of licensure.

If generic counselor licensure is slow to develop in some states, rehabilitation counselors may achieve specialized counselor licensing more readily given the longer history of their certification and accreditation processes and the more specific definition of their work.

Major Issues in Counselor Licensure

Given the newness of counselor licensure, the main issues are development of the profession's identity and relationships among the various mental health professions. As yet, there is not a clearly identifiable set of problems that most counselors and psychologists face in applying and qualifying for these forms of licensure. In fact, since the master's degree is accepted for these forms of licensure, and since the counselor licensure laws contain broad exemption and grandparent clauses, these licensing laws are not likely to be as divisive among applicants as are psychology laws, which usually require a doctorate and in some states training in clearly identified psychology departments.

However, the present lack of applicant issues does not mean that there has been great interdisciplinary harmony as these laws have developed or that no significant issues for individual counselors and psychologists will emerge. In fact, the broad exemption and grandparent clauses in the model bills resulted from challenges from the whole spectrum of mental health service providers, including ex-addict peer drug counselors and clinical psychologists.

Before discussing the interdisciplinary issues, we should briefly note issues involving professional identity that the counseling profession and its specialties have faced in pursuing licensing. Many legislators knowledgeable about occupational licensing expect standards of training, ethical codes, certification processes, and registries to be developed. The relative looseness with which the label *counselor* has been used has made fulfilling these expectations difficult; only in recent years have master's-level counselors and the rehabilitation counseling and marriage and family counseling specialists established such standards. To the extent that these codes and standards improve the quality of practitioners, licensing can help upgrade the profession, as some have argued (see Chapter Two).

Problems with definitions have inhibited the development of counselor licensure both from within and from outside the profession. The continual mutations of the definition of counseling within the profession itself were reviewed in Chapter Two. Even more so than in psychology, thousands of persons consider themselves counselors who see no need for licensing. Also, the various specialty counselors may have different views about what kind of licensing is needed. As discussed in the next chapter, getting legislation passed requires a substantial number of persons who are willing to commit themselves publicly to the entire proposed bill. Minor disagreements among groups proposing the bill give legislators the perfect excuse for not acting upon it.

Marriage and family and rehabilitation counselors have been able to implement licensure more easily because of greater agreement on definitions and needs. The emergence of the American Mental Health Counselors Association is in part related to the slow development of generic counselor licensure and registries; this group, too, may quickly develop a core of committed professionals who readily agree on standards and licensure provisions. If so, divisiveness may increase within the counseling profession as uncredentialed specialists see how fast specialty areas can establish credentialing.

Definitions have also been the source of interprofessional friction. The clearest examples have occurred between marriage and family therapists and psychologists. As mentioned earlier in this chapter, the practice of marriage and family therapy is proposed to be limited to those persons with the specified training and licensure. In many states, psychologists lobbied extensively against acts stipulating this, which eventually led to the inclusion of the grandparent clause to cover already licensed persons in allied professions. Such a provision does not, of course, cover future psychologists, who would have to gain the specified licensure in order to offer marriage and family services to the public explicitly. The interdisciplinary fighting continues in each state where marriage and family therapy licensing is proposed. Somewhat ironically, the major stimulus for developing this kind of licensing resulted from the exclusion of master's-level persons from psychology licensing. As Farmer (1979) notes, our professions hardly gain positive public images when they engage in "If you can exclude me, I can exclude you" games.

To our knowledge, no employer currently requires that counselors be licensed. Thus, the primary advantage to being licensed is that one can engage in private practice with less interference from other professions as long as one practices within the domain of the counselor licensing act. Also, this statutory recognition of the profession will probably increase recognition by federal and national oversight commissions, such as the HEW Division of Eligibility and Agency Evaluation (see Chapter Seven), thereby increasing the potential for funding of training and services. Of course, these very implications have been the driving force behind the rapidly increasing interest in counselor licensing. The early 1980s may be to the profession of counseling as the late 1960s were to psychology, when many states developed licensing for psychologists and the profession at large increasingly focused their attention on the concerns of service providers.

6

Working to Get
Legislation Enacted
or Amended

Since legislative acts are increasingly affecting the careers and functions of most psychologists and counselors, even those not engaged in private practice or receiving third-party payments, members of both professions need to learn what processes are involved in developing, changing, or, in the case of sunset regulations, simply maintaining statutory professional credentials. Even professionals seeking alternatives to licensing must know the legislative process, since all but three states currently have statutes that would need to be rescinded before alternative regulations for the psychology profession could be implemented. At the present time, relatively few psychologists and counselors know what is involved in effecting legislation satisfactory to the profession and to the public, as well as to the legislature.

This chapter reviews the important written materials for promoting legislation, as well as the observations of counselors and psychologists who have been deeply involved with legislative activities on how to implement licensure acts most effectively. Many of these persons prepared brief summaries of their experiences specifically for this book, which we incorporated in our review.

Further details on the legislative process and elaboration on the observations of the legislative activists may be found in the American Personnel and Guidance Association *Licensure Committee Action Packet* (1979) and in the very informative articles by psychologists (Dörken, 1977; Warnath, 1978) and a counselor (Witmer, 1978-1979).

The First Steps

In most cases, the implementation of a licensure action requires significant amounts of personnel, time, and money. As a result, licensure efforts by only a few interested individuals have usually failed. Unless the profession rallies in support, it is unlikely that any proposed legislation can be implemented. The history of psychological legislation, reviewed in Chapter Three, demonstrates this. Licensing proceeded slowly when one of the primary motivations was protecting the public from unauthorized persons who used the title *psychologist*. However, in states where medical practices acts restricted the psychotherapeutic services that psychologists typically offered, there was greatly increased licensure activity. Finally, in the late 1960s, when third-party reimbursement of psychologists became more possible, the development of legislation in psychology peaked.

In counseling, the key issue in every state that has implemented legislation has been the exclusion of counselors from their traditional practice by declaring them ineligible for licensing as psychologists. Arkansas's legislation for counselors was enacted more rapidly than that of almost any other state, with less than two years passing between introduction and implementation. The counselors in Arkansas reported that counselors were brought together "inadvertently . . . by the State Board of Examiners of Psychology when the board ruled that all persons providing counseling services in state agencies must hold a license to counsel. The ruling hit counselors in community mental health and social service agencies, in rehabilitation centers and mental hospitals. Many counselors were given notice to comply with the ruling within two years or risk losing employment" ("Arkansas to License Counselors," 1979, p. 1).

The situation in Kansas was quite different. During 1979, a review and audit of the psychological board of examiners prompted praise for its careful work but chiding for the self-serving manner of its operations, particularly in its exclusion of applicants for licensure. The auditor, who had also reviewed the board of social work examiners, recommended to the legislature that it abolish both boards and establish a new omnibus board whose functions would include the examination and credentialing of psychologists, social workers, and mental health service providers (J. Lichtenberg, personal communication, 1979).

Once an issue has been identified that elicits the support of the profession, a series of steps must be taken before the legislature is consulted.

What Legislators Ask

The next step is to learn what legislative experts believe should be included in professional regulations. The most important literature on this subject is the booklet *Occupational Licensing: Questions a Legislature Should Ask* (Shimberg and Roederer, 1978). The authors, knowledgeable about occupational regulations, worked with the Council of State Governments to obtain information on licensing, including whether state governments should regulate occupational groups at all, how to draft regulatory statutes that are fair to practitioners and consumers alike, and how to establish an administrative structure that promotes accountability and public confidence. Many of the guidelines in the following list are self-explanatory. Full descriptions of the guidelines are provided in the booklet, which is available from the Council of State Governments (address in appendix).

The guidelines are as follows:

1. Regulations should meet a public need.
2. Government regulations should be minimal.

3. If an occupation is to be licensed, its scope of practice should be coordinated with restrictions due to existing statutes to avoid fragmentation and inefficiency in the delivery of services.
4. Requirements and evaluation procedures for entry into an occupation should clearly relate to safe and effective practice.
5. Every out-of-state licensee or applicant should have fair and reasonable access to the credentialing process.
6. Once granted, a credential should remain valid as long as the holder can provide evidence of competence.
7. The public should be involved in the regulatory process.
8. Complaints should be investigated and resolved in a manner that is satisfactory and creditable to the public.
9. Procedures for evaluating the qualifications of applicants and disciplinary proceedings against licensees should be conducted in a fair manner.
10. The purpose of regulation is to protect the public, not the economic interest of the occupational group.
11. The administrative structure should provide efficiency, policy coordination, and public accountability.
12. The system used to finance regulatory activities should contribute to the accountability of individual boards and to the effectiveness of the overall regulatory program (Shimberg and Roederer, 1978).

This same booklet includes an extensive list of questions that legislators typically ask about professional licensing bills. Since these questions provide an outstanding guide to anyone faced with the task of testifying on behalf of professional legislation, they are presented below in their entirety, courtesy of the Council of State Governments. By having answers to all of these questions, any person proposing new or modified licensure regulations would be well prepared and therefore gain more credibility from the legislators, as well as be able to testify with less anxiety than is usually found at such sessions.

What Is the Problem? 1) Has the public been harmed because the occupational group has not been regulated? 1a) To what extent has the public's health, safety, or economic well-being been harmed? 2) Can the claims of proponents of regulation be documented?

Why Should the Occupation Group Be Regulated? 1) Who are the users of services offered? 1a) Are they members of the general public who lack knowledge necessary to evaluate qualifications of those offering services? 1b) Are they institutions or qualified professionals who have the knowledge to evaluate qualifications? 2) What is the extent of autonomy of practitioners? 2a) Is there a high degree of independent judgment required of practitioners? 2b) How much skill and experience are required in making these judgments? 2c) Do practitioners customarily work on their own or under supervision? 2d) If supervised, is supervisor covered by regulatory statute?

What Efforts Have Been Made to Address the Problems? 1) Has the occupational group established a code of ethics? 1a) To what extent has it been accepted and enforced? 2) Has the occupational group established complaint-handling procedures for resolving disputes between practitioners and public? 2a) How effective has this been? 3) Has a nongovernmental certification program been established to assist the public in identifying qualified practitioners? 4) Could the use of applicable laws or existing standards solve problems? 4a) Use of unfair and deceptive trade practices laws. 4b) Use of civil laws such as injunctions, cease and desist orders, and so on. 4c) Use of criminal laws such as prohibitions against cheating, false pretenses, deceptive advertising, and so on. 4d) Use of existing standards such as construction codes, product safety standards, and so on. 5) Would strengthened existing laws or standards help to deal with the problem?

Have Alternatives to Licensure Been Considered? 1) Use of an existing agency under legislative control. 2) Regulation of business employer rather than individual practitioner, for example, licensing restaurants rather than cooks or waiters/waitresses. 3) Registration of practitioners coupled with minimum standards set by state agency. 4) Certification of practitioners, thereby restricting use of title to those who have demonstrated competence. Occupational groups, however, would not have control of field of practice. 5) Why would the use of the above not be adequate to protect the public interest? 5a) Why would licensing be more effective?

Will the Public Benefit from Regulation of the Occupation? 1) How will regulation help public identify qualified practitioners? 2) How will regulation assure that practitioners are competent? 2a) What standards are proposed for granting credentials? 2b) Are all standards job related? 2c) How do these standards compare with those of other states? 2d) If standards differ from those of other states, can the difference be justified? 2e) Are there training and experience requirements? Are these requirements of excessive duration when compared with other states? Why? Does training include supervised field experience? If so, is an additional experience requirement justified? 2f) Are there restrictions on where or how experience may be acquired? Why? 2g) Will alternative routes of entry be recognized? Will applicants who have not gone through prescribed training/experience be eligible for licensure or certification? Will licensure or certification in another state automatically allow an individual to be credentialed in this state? 2h) Will applicants for licensure or certification be required to pass an examination? Does an examination already exist? Does it meet professional and legal testing standards? If no test exists, who will develop it and how will development cost be met? 2i) Is there a "grandfather" clause in licensure? Why is it necessary? Will such practitioners be required to take a test at a later date? 3) What assurance will the public have that the individuals credentialed by the state have maintained their competence? 3a) Will license or certificate carry expiration date? 3b) Will renewal be based solely on payment of fee? 3c) Will renewal require periodic examination, peer review, evidence of continuing education, or other procedures for continued competence? 4) How will complaints of the public against practitioners be handled? 4a) Will there be a method for receiving complaints? 4b) Will there be an effective procedure for disciplining incompetent or unethical practitioners? 4c) What grounds will there be for suspension or revocation of credentials? 5) Is it feasible to establish a restitution fund so that the public will be able to recover money lost through actions of unscrupulous practitioners?

Will Regulation Be Harmful to the Public? 1) Will competition be restricted by the occupational group, for example, prohibiting price advertising? 2) Will the occupational group control the supply of practitioners? 2a) By standards more restrictive than necessary? 2b) By restricting entry of those from other states who have substantially similar qualifications? 3) Will regulation prevent the optimum utilization of personnel? 3a) Will "scope of practice" prevent individuals from other occupational groups from providing services for which they are qualified by training and experience? 4) Will regulation increase costs of goods and services to consumers? 5) Will regulation decrease availability of practitioners? 6) Are there safeguards in law to ensure that the occupational group does not use its powers to promote self-interest over those of public?

How Will the Regulatory Activity Be Administered? 1) Will the regulatory entity be composed only of members of occupation? 1a) Will there be public members on the regulatory entity? In what percentage? 2) What powers will regulatory entity have? 2a) Will it review qualifications, examinations, investigations, and disciplining of practitioners? 2b) Will it promulgate rules and codes of conduct? 3) Will actions of regulatory entity be subject to review? 3a) By whom? 3b) Will reviewing authority have power to override regulatory entity actions? Which ones? 4) How would cost of administering regulatory entity be financed? 4a) How will fees be set? 4b) Will income from fees go into general fund, departmental fund, or special account controlled by regulatory entity?

Who Is Sponsoring the Regulatory Program? 1) Are members of the public sponsoring regulatory program? 2) What associations, organizations, or other groups in the state represent practitioners? 2a) Approximately how many practitioners belong to each group? 2b) What are the different levels of practice in each group? 3) Which of the above groups are actively involved in sponsoring regulatory programs? 3a) Are other groups supporting the effort? If not, why?

Why Is Regulation Being Sought? 1) Is the occupational group seeking to enhance its status by having its own regulatory law? 2) Is the occupational group claiming it is prevented from rendering services for which its members are qualified by "scope of practice" statement of another occupation? 2a) If so, what efforts have been made to resolve differences? 3) Is the occupational group seeking licensure in order to gain reimbursement under federal-state programs or private insurers, for example, Medicare or Blue Cross? 4) Is the public seeking greater accountability of the occupational group? [Shimberg and Roederer, 1978, pp. 15-18].

Witmer (1978-1979) has provided fairly extensive responses to many of these questions. Although answers will vary from state to state, as he acknowledges, his suggestions will save counselors a great deal of time in formulating responses. A few of Witmer's responses are provided in the following paragraphs. Some of his responses may be quite controversial, especially among psychologists; nonetheless, legislators readily acknowledge, indeed expect, that issues regarding who can practice are a major reason for professional regulation.

Witmer's response to the question "What is the problem?" is as follows: "While counseling as a profession does exist, it has no legal recognition or definition. Anyone can use the title 'counselor' and hold himself/herself out to the public as providing 'counseling services'. . . . Counselors are being denied employment in the human, health, and social services because they are not appropriately licensed or certified. . . . State boards of psychology have increasingly refused to permit individuals trained outside departments of psychology to take the state licensure examination, even though the applicant's educational program has been 'primarily psychological in nature' " (1978-1979, #3, pp. 2-3).

In response to the question "Why should the occupation group be regulated?" Witmer suggests: "The process of counseling is essentially an interpersonal relationship which involves the client's mental health, life style, and personal development. Persons, not products, are at stake. In most states barbers and beauticians are required to complete classroom instruction and, in some states, as many as 1500 clock hours of experience, to qualify for licensure. How does one explain there being no minimum requirements for counselors who help people get their heads together and chart their own destiny?" (1978-1979, #3, p. 4).

In response to the question "Why is regulation being sought?" Witmer cites the policies of the American Psychological Association and the Veterans Administration that are being used to restrict the employment of counselors who have traditionally filled certain roles, as well as the policies of the Department of Health, Education, and Welfare calling for national certification for health professionals and the policies of several government agencies limiting reimbursements for services to licensed individuals. In responding to the question "Have alternatives to licensure been considered?": "Loss of licensure would effectively be loss of livelihood by loss of insurance reimbursement, inability to provide forensic services or workers' compensation services, inability to hold hospital staff membership or privileges, loss of privileged communication, loss of the ability to form a professional corporation, and inability to purchase professional liability (malpractice) insurance. Moreover, delicensure of psychology would end their services to Medicaid beneficiaries, reestablish a psychiatric monopoly, and increase costs to the state" (p. 3).

Witmer notes that whenever counselors have attempted to use existing legislative controls, related professional associations have vigorously objected. In responding to the question "Will regulation be harmful to the public?" Witmer responds that standards in the recommended bill are not overly exclusive or restrictive and that other occupational groups are not restricted or prevented from providing services for which they are qualified by training and experience. He also suggests that the regulation will stabilize but not reduce the cost of services to consumers by providing additional mental health professionals.

Psychologists may wish to note that Dörken (1979) has responded to this question from a very different perspective concerning the potential danger of sunset legislation.

Organizational Steps: First Phase

The next step in developing or modifying licensure is the appointment of a licensure committee. Several factors must be considered in selecting members of the committee. Although interest is important, each member should be able to spend as much as six to ten hours a week on licensure issues and be prepared to serve a minimum of one and preferably two years. Without this time commitment, the work cannot be done. Also, if committee members constantly change, the beginning steps will be repeated by each new committee, and it will be difficult to get past the preliminary steps. If members serve for only one year, new members should be groomed toward the end of the year and serve simultaneously with the retiring members. The committee, which should consist of six to ten persons, should also represent the different job settings, specialties, levels of training, genders, and ethnic backgrounds of the constituency of the organization. Such broad representation assures broad-based support for the proposals.

The chairperson of such a group should be able to gain the trust of the profession's or sponsoring organization's members, because he or she will often have to act on behalf of the sponsors without consulting them first. If the chair does not have this trust, each such action will become a major impediment rather than a facilitating step toward licensure. Good listening, empathic responding, the ability to compromise, assertiveness, and communication and support skills have all been identified as qualities needed by the chairperson (Witmer, 1978-1979).

Once a licensure committee is established, each member must learn the licensure and credentialing issues of their profession in their state. All the material covered in this book should be familiar, and it should be supplemented by reading from within their own professions. At this point full responses must be reviewed for the legislators' anticipated questions. Other questions must also be answered like the following: "Approximately how many persons will be eligible during the grandfathering period?" "How much will it cost the state to maintain the board that regulates the profession?" Additionally, at this point the committee should review the difficulties that members of other professions have had in developing licensure and the difficulties that the sponsoring profession's members have had in being licensed by existing state boards. The attitudes of the legislators toward the creation of new licensing boards and the activities of sunset commissions should be determined.

After this information is obtained (and if the committee still believes that licensure is desirable), the committee should prepare a position paper that addresses the needs of the group's membership and of the public. It is critical that this position paper, once it has the full support of the licensure committee, be circulated to all members of the sponsoring organization before a draft bill is prepared. The committee should anticipate which parts of the position paper might elicit resistance from within the profession. If the profession does not present a united front to the public and the legislature, it is highly unlikely that both the legislature and the governor will approve any proposal.

At this point contact with other professions should be seriously considered, both those that might support the legislation and those that might object to it (this step will be explored more fully in the next section). The committee may determine possible opposition before a draft bill is written. However, some have argued that one should not arouse these possible opponents needlessly, and that the type of opposition is fairly predictable from a review of licensure efforts in other states. No definitive guideline exists on this point at this time.

Once the vast majority of the profession has endorsed the position paper and all opposition within the profession has been minimized, a draft bill should be written. This involves recasting the position paper into legislative language; various publications by psychological and counselor organizations are useful here, as are copies of bills from states that have already enacted such legislation (see Chapters Three and Five).

If the licensing committee represents the diversity of the profession, there should be no problem in gaining cooperation from all groups within the profession. If the committee is not fully representative, input from unrepresented constituencies should be carefully solicited. Have persons teaching in the field as well as those practicing in the field been consulted? What about those in administrative settings? In remote locations? Each of these constituencies may have concerns that were overlooked by urban practitioners, who are typically involved in the preparation of licensing position papers.

The final step of the first phase is to educate the membership intensively through newsletter articles, state convention programs, membership surveys, and brochures on licensure. The draft bill needs to become a focal point of the profession. After enough time has elapsed to receive and incorporate feedback into the draft bill, the executive body of a sponsoring organization should adopt the bill. The licensing committee should be empowered to make additional changes if political and legislative exigencies so dictate.

Organizational Steps: Second Phase

The second and final phase before the legislative process ideally involves everyone in the profession. The profession must be prepared for the legislative process and the role that each member must adopt. At least three steps must be undertaken in this phase. A membership communication network must be established that provides quick, effective, two-way communication between members and leaders. A tree-type organization is preferable; at the top should be a few key statewide leaders, and under them should be regional coordinators, district representatives, local representatives, and finally local members. People should be designated to contact every member in the organization, and every member should know which local professional representative he or she should contact. If the legislative phase should demand urgent action, such a network allows most of the profession to be reached in a very short period of time, providing the opportunity for professionals to contact every legislator in the state.

Second, to help members understand their roles and to represent the bill properly, materials should be developed that describe what licensure will do and how it can best be presented to the public, other professions, and legislators. Local and regional workshops can also be very effective in educating the profession.

Third, other mental health professional groups should be informed of legislative plans and solicited for feedback and support. Especially critical is contact with groups that will support the bill. Community mental health workers of various professions and educational levels, clinical social workers, and state office representatives of the profession have usually been quite supportive of licensing in psychology and counseling. Lay mental health organizations and consumer protection groups should also be contacted for support.

Other recommended steps in this phase include preparing a detailed budget so that the licensure effort does not run out of funds. Recent counselor licensure efforts have cost as little as $600 and as much as $20,000. If a professional lobbyist is employed, which almost every group that has recently attempted licensure highly recommends, the cost could be considerably higher. Expenses include printing, postage, telephones, travel, meals, and dining with legislators. This last item is not a way of buying votes but rather to get the attention of legislators so that personal relationships can be established and the profession's credibility increased.

At this point, Witmer (1978-1979) suggests that the licensure committee review its skills in conflict resolution. It is also important that the committee review and agree on how much it can compromise without seriously affecting the standards proposed or losing the support of the profession. Finally, the committee must be prepared to face the inevitable crises. "Misunderstandings, false information, inadequate information, or outdated information are frequently responsible for sudden changes in the position persons or groups take in relation to the bill. Waiting to oppose a bill at a crucial point in legislative hearings is part of the strategy of some groups. The element of surprise gives the proponents little time to counter the opposition prior to the committee or floor vote. . . . Crises may occur when there are sudden changes in legislative committee plans for hearing the bill or when legislators change votes or earlier stated positions on the bill" (Witmer, 1978-1979, #2, p. 5).

The committee must realize that from this point forward licensing is primarily a political process (Warnath, 1978). Negotiations and compromises will now be based on getting the bill passed rather than what makes good sense for consumers or the profession. Grandparent clauses are often a sore point at this stage, since those proposing the licensing bill often find that the bill can only pass if some persons are licensed to whom they would never trust the welfare of the client (Warnath, 1978).

At this point the profession may have to collaborate with one or more other professions. If significant resistance is expected, it may be worthwhile to join with other mental health or health professions to propose an omnibus bill. Coalitions of psychologists, social workers, and counselors may seek to establish an omnibus board overseeing specialty boards. This is happening in Kansas, where psychologists and social workers stand to lose their licensing acts. In practice, most coalitions develop only after a licensing bill has already failed, but this route should be considered beforehand if it may be helpful in gaining licensure. Such coalitions may involve so many people that passage becomes much easier. For example, in Ohio, where social workers and counselors are collaborating to submit a single bill, over 18,000 professional persons would be covered; this is a very substantial group of educated voters, which would have impact on a state legislature.

Finally, the licensing committee must realize that a state, not a national, political process is involved. While national standards and national documents may have been used in drafting the bill and developing a rationale, they must not be emphasized. Each state legislature jealously guards its own autonomy in implementing laws. What is good for the state of Iowa may not at all appeal to legislators of Kansas!

Legislative Actions

Once the bill is ready to be introduced to the legislature, the first and most important action is to obtain sponsors of the bill in both houses, preferably the most powerful individuals. These sponsors should be members of the majority party or respected by both parties and have a good record in getting licensure bills passed. After selecting the legislators for introducing the bill, the licensing committee must sell the sponsors on the importance of licensure and express willingness to accept input from the legislators in the final writing of the bill. Past experience shows that a mildly receptive but powerful sponsor is a better choice than an enthusiastic but relatively weak one.

Person-to-person contacts with legislators become critical at this point. Ideally, before legislative sessions begin, members of the profession who are fully informed about the bill will visit the home offices of legislators. Legislators have more time at their home offices than they do during legislative sessions to talk about the bill. If possible, these contacts should be made by persons who already know the legislators, but it is important that as many legislators be contacted as possible, even if members of the profession must meet with legislators whom they have never met. A good contact with an unacquainted legislator may be worth as much if not more than a contact with a legislator who knows the profession. Members of the profession should be stationed in the lounge and hallways of the statehouse, possibly arranging lunches or dinners with legislators, in order to maintain contacts. A brief encounter in a hallway can involve social amenities as well as a reminder of interest in the progress of the proposed legislation.

It is especially important that these later contacts be preceded by or occur simultaneously with an extensive letter-writing campaign; hopefully every legislator in the state will have received letters from persons in his or her jurisdiction that support the legislation. The communications network outlined in the preceding section should be used to telephone every single member of the profession and to urge them to write (on their own stationery) to their legislators. The gist of these letters should be "I want you, as my area's legislator, to support this bill." To increase the likelihood of every member writing a letter, the licensure committee can provide a form letter to each member that can be signed and sent to the legislator. This is better than no response at all but clearly a poor second to sending a personalized letter. Also, each member must be provided with the names and addresses of the legislators to whom she or he should write. Dörken (1979) found that most California psychologists knew none of the names of their legislators.

When the bill is about to be voted on, a last-minute campaign should be waged to gain the support of legislators who are undecided or against the bill, as determined by the licensure committee. Mailgrams or Personal Opinion Messages from Western Union are relatively inexpensive ($2.00 to $3.00 each) and are delivered within approximately twenty-four hours. A burst of such communications will remind the legislators of past correspondence as well as provide evidence of the continuing strong interest by their constituents.

Experienced professionals have also pointed out the need for the team providing the testimony at the legislative hearings to be well prepared. Ideally this team should consist of the most prominent professionals in the state, persons who have some public standing as researchers or developers of well-accepted service programs. If such persons cannot be obtained, significant administrators of state universities or major professional services should be sought. The licensing committee should fully inform these persons about the bill itself, expected opposition, and responses to legislators' questions.

Legislators are often particularly persuaded by testimony from someone whose practice has been prohibited or restricted by another occupational board. Such testimony from a well trained and previously established professional may persuade legislators that fair play is needed to prevent a board from restricting the services offered by another profession.

Witmer (1978-1979) has nicely summarized many important points on preparing legislative testimony. When possible, the most knowledgeable and prominent persons from the team should testify first. All members of the team need to know the protocol of the legislature, such as how to address the chair, committee members, and the like. Before testifying, team members need to identify themselves, their areas of expertise, and the interests that they represent.

Witmer (1978-1979) adds that the testimony should be completely written out for the legislators, but presented orally from notes rather than read. It should focus on the problem and why regulations are needed. It should *not* include attacks on other professional groups. While delivering the testimony, good eye contact with legislators is as important as it is in interviews. People who testify later should be aware of what has already been stated and be careful not to repeat the same information. Each person's testimony should end with a very brief summary and an offer to answer any questions.

The legislative testimony is ideally followed by a session for the profession's licensure committee to assess how well they presented their testimony and how to follow up on any questions by the legislators that were not answered as well as the team might like.

Warnath (1978) has pointed out something that too many professionals have learned the hard way—the need to monitor the bill daily. Once the bill has been submitted, the profession's licensure committee loses control over what gets attached, deleted, or modified. So that the profession is not surprised a few weeks after the bill is submitted, at least one person should monitor it daily from its submission until the governor's signature.

As counselors in Arkansas learned, the monitoring and campaign of support must be maintained until the governor actually signs the bill, even after the legislature passes the bill. In this state, an aide to the governor supported the objections of alcohol and drug abuse counselors to the counselor licensure bill and was developing support to veto the bill, which had been passed by the legislature. By having the bill recalled to the senate floor and thereby preventing the veto since the bill was out of the governor's office, the licensure committee gained the time necessary to allay the fears of the opposition ("Arkansas to License Counselors," 1979). Obviously, only after the governor signs the bill is it time to break out the champagne!

While many of the details of this chapter are of value only to those who develop or promote legislation, all members of the profession who are concerned about licensing developments must realize the time, effort, funds, and commitment by each member that are necessary. If you care, you must take part. When only a few persons are involved, no matter how knowledgeable and skilled they are, it is difficult, if not impossible, for legislative actions to be successful.

$$\equiv\!\!\!\Rightarrow\!0\!\Leftarrow\!\!\Rightarrow\!0\!\Leftarrow \quad 7 \quad \equiv\!\!\!\Rightarrow\!0\!\Leftarrow\!\!\Rightarrow\!0\!\Leftarrow$$

Accreditation of Education, Training, and Service Programs

The preceding chapters have discussed legislation for licensing and certifying psychologists and counselors. In addition to such statutory recognition, many other accrediting bodies and other forms of credentialing (typically voluntary) exist. This chapter reviews those organizations and agencies that accredit education, training, and service programs, giving special attention to the implications of program accreditation for counselors and psychologists, and the problems that counselors and psychologists typically encounter in dealing with these organizations and agencies.

Program accreditations have several advantages and disadvantages. The general purpose of most program accreditations is to promote and ensure the quality of the training or services provided. Truly irresponsible training and services are not accredited, thereby providing some protection for consumers, whether clients or students. Accreditation also enables the student or professional to join a program of recognized quality, and some licensing and credentialing agencies certify degrees from approved programs almost automatically. In the employment market, persons who have been trained or have served in accredited programs and agencies are often selected over those who lack such experience. Accreditation also provides the accredited body with evaluation and feedback from other professionals.

Counterbalancing these positive aspects are some rarely discussed drawbacks. Although accreditation does protect the consumer against irresponsible services and training, some institutions believe that the constraints that accreditation entails intrude into their autonomy. As a result, some institutions do not seek accreditation. Thus, a program that is not accredited by an accrediting agency is not necessarily of low quality. On the other hand, programs that are accredited have been judged by professionals as meeting their specified goals and objectives.

Students, trainees, and employees often feel that accreditation places constraints on the content and procedures of their training or service programs that may be unproductive. Most accrediting agencies have explicit requirements pertaining to the credentials of those who supervise, affirmative action, and, increasingly, content areas and types of experience. These requirements often limit a program's options. For example, they might prevent a student from an internship that may be very pertinent to his or her planned career but that lacks an appropriately credentialed supervisor. Or an innovative service may not be established because its designated leader might not meet accreditation guidelines. In these situations, the trainee or professional will not only feel the constraint of the accreditation requirements but also find that administrators will balk at any proposal that would threaten accreditation.

Accreditation typically requires a significant amount of information about the training or service setting, which is compiled periodically, often every year. This information ranges

from a review of the conceptual bases of the program to detailed data on who entered, received what training, or provided
what service, to an evaluation of services. Professional personnel
in service settings and students in training programs often assist
in compiling these data and meet with the site visitors of the
accreditation body. A major issue for any administrator in preparing for site visits is how much to attempt to look good and
how candid to be.

Accreditation of Training Programs and Internships by the American Psychological Association

The American Psychological Association (APA) accredits
university graduate training programs in clinical, counseling, and
school psychology as well as combinations of these programs.
The APA also accredits internship training in those areas. The
purpose of the accreditation is to promote excellent programs
designed to educate professional psychologists and to provide a
professional and objective evaluation of these programs.

The APA has been accrediting doctoral programs since
the 1940s in clinical psychology, the 1950s in counseling, and
the 1960s in school psychology. In late 1979, there were 117
approved programs in clinical psychology, 25 in counseling
psychology, 12 in school psychology, and 3 in combined scientific-professional programs. Internships have been evaluated
since 1956; a total of 171 had been approved as of late 1979.

Accreditation policies and procedures have been continually revised to keep abreast of the changes in professional
psychology. The current guidelines, which apply to all programs
as of September 1, 1980, were approved in January 1979 after
several years of controversial deliberations dealing with (1) the
problems for accreditation presented by the increasing number
of professional psychology schools (as compared to traditional
departments of psychology), (2) issues of affirmative action,
and (3) religious discrimination.

The criteria for accreditation of training and internship
programs are briefly summarized in the following paragraphs.
Special attention has been given to specific course content and

personnel requirements. Anyone interested in developing an accredited program or in obtaining more details on any of the criteria should write to the APA Office of Accreditation (address in appendix) and request the "Criteria for Accreditation of Doctoral Training Programs and Internships in Professional Psychology."

Criteria for Accreditation of Doctoral Training Programs

Institutional Settings. To be eligible for accreditation, programs must meet the criteria for psychology programs described in Chapter Three of this book *and* demonstrate that the institution provides appropriate financial support to the program.

Cultural and Individual Differences. "Social responsibility and respect for cultural and individual differences are attitudes which must be imparted to students and trainees and be reflected in all phases of the program operation: faculty recruitment and promotion, student recruitment and evaluation, curriculum, and field training" (American Psychological Association, 1979, p. 4). Students must gain knowledge and skills "relevant to human diversity such as people with handicapping conditions; of differing ages, genders, ethnic and racial backgrounds, religions, and life styles; and from differing social and individual backgrounds" (p. 4).

Training Models and Curriculum. Theory and research are to be integrated early in the program. Students should form an early identification with their profession, and they must demonstrate competence in the biological, cognitive-affective, social, and individual bases of behavior. Training is required in skills related to specialty areas, such as psychological assessment and program evaluation. Students must be knowledgeable about and value professional ethics and scientific responsibility and integrity.

Research training should include a variety of methodological paradigms, and the student should be free to choose research topics that are relevant to his or her training and appropriate to the profession of psychology. A "diversity of philosophies, goals, and practices from program to program and from individual student to individual student must be permitted. Each program must specify its training model and goal in writing . . . . Programs are evaluated in terms of the model endorsed, the goals stated and the success in meeting these goals" (American Psychological Association, 1979, p. 9).

Faculty. The faculty must include experienced, productive persons who can provide effective leadership, modeling, supervision, and instruction; have a sound background of training experience, including a psychology internship where appropriate; and show evidence of staying abreast of developments in their field.

Students.

> The intellectual and personal characteristics of students, how they are selected, the nature of their interactions with faculty, and the manner in which students are helped by faculty in achieving their goals are factors to be evaluated. In addition to intellectual ability, students of professional psychology should have a commitment to social justice and to contributing to the well being of others. . . . A full description of the program, to be sent to all applicants, should include the program's theoretical orientation; the professional functions for which the student will be prepared; professional and research interests of faculty members; the usual size of the applicant pool; the acceptance and attrition rates; the percentage of male, female, minority, and handicapped students; students' age distribution; the availability and nature of financial, academic, counseling, and other support systems; requirements for full-time and part-time student status; and information about local living conditions. . . . Faculty have special responsibility to assess continually the progress of each student. . . . There should be specific advisement policies and mechanisms . . . to handle academic problems, conflict situations, and problems related to expectations, interpersonal relations and other areas [American Psychological Association, 1979, pp. 13-14].

Facilities. Teaching facilities, library facilities, office space, work space, research, relevant materials and supplies, practicum and internship facilities, data analysis facilities, audiovisual equipment, research equipment, and facilities for handicapped students should all be evaluated.

Practicum and Internship Training. "Practicum training should begin as early as feasible in the doctoral training program. The experiences of students should be appropriate to their level of training. Choice of particular facilities should be based primarily upon their quality and their relevance to the training objectives of the program. The training should be coordinated by an active faculty member, or by an adjunct professor associated with the practicum facility. The minimum practicum experience is 400 hours, of which at least 150 hours is in direct service experience and at least 75 hours in formally scheduled supervision" (American Psychological Association, 1979, pp. 17-18).

Criteria for Accreditation of Independent Internship Centers

Internships are to be offered only to those students who have completed relevant didactic and practium work for the doctoral degree; internships should be intensive, extensive experiences that increase the knowledge, skills, and sensitivities developed in the practica.

"Internships in clinical psychology require full-time experience either for one calendar year, or for two years at half-time experience, and may or may not be in a single agency. School and counseling psychology internships require a full-time experience for either the academic or the calendar year or half-time experience for two years" (American Psychological Association, 1979, pp. 18-19).

There must be evidence of administrative support for the program in terms of resources and budgeting for training operations; the internship program and the graduate program of the student must establish regular communication with each other; sites must conform to all relevant APA standards and guidelines and demonstrate a high regard for human dignity.

The professional psychology staff should be sufficiently large to provide a variety of role models; while primary emphasis should be on the training by professional psychologists, collaborative work with representatives of other disciplines is desirable.

Interns' preparation should be carefully reviewed. "Efforts should be made to select students from APA-approved doctoral programs in the relevant area of professional psychology. Doctoral psychologists who are attempting to qualify as practitioners in an area different from their original training areas must be certified by a director of graduate professional psychology training as having participated in an organized program in which the equivalent of pre-internship preparation has been acquired. Applicants from programs awarding degrees in areas other than psychology shall not be accepted as interns" (American Psychological Association, 1979, p. 21).

An agency should be able to provide for more than two interns in any given setting, and interns should be actively involved in evaluating their own experiences. The program should be thoroughly described in materials sent to applicants, provide supervised experience in an organized sequence of activities and exposure to a variety of problems, ensure that interns learn and apply ethical standards in their practice, and provide intensive individual supervision at least two hours a week, as well as group learning experiences (American Psychological Association, 1979).

*Problems in Qualifying for Accreditation
as an Educational Program*

This section describes those criteria that programs have the most difficulty in meeting, and it suggests how students and faculty can help their programs to pass these requirements.

The requirement that every program offer an integrated, organized plan of study essentially excludes programs in which courses may be freely chosen or in which doctoral candidates can receive credit for courses taken at different schools over an extended period of time. The typical approved program will clearly specify a set of minimum courses or competencies as well as recommended electives.

The requirement that a program demonstrate responsiveness to cultural and individual differences is new to the 1979 criteria; many programs now need to develop and document offerings that meet this criterion. It will hardly suffice to say, "We cover cultural diversity in our standard courses."

While most programs describe their training program with reasonable thoroughness, they often lack a quality control mechanism that guarantees that all students have sufficient breadth and depth; a well-designed program can specify such a mechanism.

Programs must carefully attend to the qualifications of their faculty. The placement of any faculty members not trained in the area of specialization applied for but who train students in this area must be justified with appropriate documentation.

Affirmative action with respect to both student and faculty selection needs to be documented; simply stating that no discrimination exists does not satisfy the criterion of cultural diversity.

The specification of the number of hours of direct service and supervision required in practica is new to the 1979 criteria. Applying programs or students must document these figures.

Both counseling and school psychology programs are often offered by departments or divisions of a university outside of the department of psychology. Such a program is evaluated in two other areas: the program's fulfillment of the psychology components in terms of both content and personnel, and a statement of the program's mission. For a program housed outside of a psychology department, the course content and the credentials of the instructors are usually reviewed more carefully than those for programs housed in psychology departments. Is a course in biological psychology taught in a human development department equivalent to such a course taught in a psychology department, or is it more narrowly defined and possibly insufficiently psychological in nature? Are persons teaching in a guidance and counseling program who received their degrees from such a program and who are not licensed as psychologists appropriate instructors for a counseling psychology course? In 1976 the Council of Counseling Psychology Training Programs identified over seventy programs in which at least one faculty member was interested in training counseling psychologists at the doctoral level; however, fewer than thirty of these programs had either APA approval or administrative support for developing an approved program.

In defining program mission, counseling psychologists more than clinical and school psychologists have often felt pushed into a defensive position. Discussions of the differentiation between clinical and counseling psychology have filled many pages since the establishment of the APA Division of Counseling Psychology in 1952. The lack of a consensus by practitioners and leaders of the profession, documents such as the Grayston Report (Thompson and Super, 1964) notwithstanding, has often caused site visitors to question whether a particular counseling psychology program was providing training that was conceptually different from that provided by clinical psychology. This question becomes especially pertinent if the campus already has a clinical psychology program. Would the expansion of the clinical program be economically more feasible than the development of a separately approved program? The fact that some counseling psychology programs have been abandoned in the last decade because of this vague distinction has accentuated this issue as has the regrettable tendency of graduates from counseling psychology programs to identify themselves as clinical psychologists soon after graduating (Cleveland, 1979).

The mission and course offerings of programs seeking combined scientific-professional accreditation experience are also scrutinized. Of course, before applying for accreditation, such programs should have a well-developed mission statement accepted by all of their faculty.

The psychology course work of programs housed outside of psychology departments is often offered through psychology departments. In such cases, special attention is given to whether students can be readily admitted to those courses. A program would get a poor review if students could not fulfill certain course requirements outside of their department in a normal sequence because they were on a waiting list to get into those courses.

Problems in Qualifying for Accreditation
as an Internship Program

As stated earlier, the training institution must demonstrate a commitment to training and not simply be using interns as cheap labor, that is, asking a great deal of service without providing either adequate supervision or other learning experiences such as case conferences and research. Pressure for heavy service commitments is greatest in public service agencies, which are often under pressure to show that most of their time allotment is used for direct service.

The amount and quality of supervision are often stumbling blocks to accreditation. The 1979 criteria prescribe the minimum required amount of supervision, which some agencies had not observed in the past: two hours of formally scheduled individual supervision per week. A high-quality internship frequently provides as much as four to six hours of individual supervision per week plus participation in diagnostic case conferences, in-service training groups for all staff, and the like. To provide adequate role modeling, primary supervisors must generally be psychologists rather than persons from other professions such as social work or guidance counseling. Even those trained as psychologists are expected to be licensed or certified by the state or province, as appropriate.

Many small agencies with limited staff or resources have difficulty meeting the criterion that more than two interns must be in a program. Exceptions are rare unless there is very strong evidence of a very high quality training program in all other respects.

There have been some problems in accrediting internship settings in clinical and counseling psychology. Before 1973, counseling psychology and clinical psychology internships were differentiated. After 1973, there was sufficient agreement that the two internship settings were similar enough to have the single designation "internships in professional psychology." As a result, counseling psychology students could intern in community mental health centers that had previously been approved only as clinical settings, and clinical psychology students could intern in university counseling centers. As specialty desig-

nations have become more of an issue (see Chapter Three and
the section on specialty standards in this chapter), renewed
attention has been given to whether an agency considers its program suitable for both counseling and clinical interns. Is there a
justifiable common program? If so, interns from either specialty
may be admitted. However, if the agency specifies different
"tracks" for counseling and clinical interns, then according to
the 1979 APA criteria, trainees are limited to the track relevant
to their graduate training *unless* the director of the other track
program determines that the graduate training of the applicant
is equivalent to the type required.

Seeking Help for APA Accreditation

Several associations can assist programs or individuals
wanting to develop or maintain accreditation of training facilities. For general information on developing an accredited program, the APA Office of Accreditation has a packet of materials
that describe the usual sequence of steps. Once a program that
has decided to seek approval has collected information demon-
strating its importance and stability, a "pre-site" visitor is
recommended. Such a visitor is a consultant brought in by the
agency to review and evaluate the program and to inform the
agency about any areas in which its program does not meet the
criteria for accreditation. The Office of Accreditation can provide a list of knowledgeable consultants.

Concerns about the appropriateness of APA accreditation
criteria should be addressed to the Education and Training
Board of the APA, which is responsible for developing and jus-
tifying any changes in the criteria. Concerns about policies of
assessing how a program meets the criteria should be addressed
to the APA Committee on Accreditation; however, we realize
that students and faculty often feel like David versus Goliath in
challenging or questioning the Committee on Accreditation. The
clinical, counseling, and school divisions of the APA and the
council of training directors of each of these specialties willingly
explain and clarify accreditation procedures. For university and
college counseling centers with concerns about accreditation,

the recently formed Association of Counseling Center Training Agencies should be helpful. Contact persons and addresses for these organizations can be obtained from the APA Educational Affairs Office (address in appendix).

Implications of Program Accreditation for Individuals

Completion of an APA-approved training or internship program has three advantages. First, as already noted, approved internships are to give preference to applicants from APA-approved training programs. (Related to this is a subject that may be confusing to counseling psychology students—internships funded by the National Institute of Mental Health [NIMH]. NIMH training funds are restricted to graduates of APA-approved clinical psychology programs or students from other training programs [counseling psychology, developmental psychology, or community psychology] funded by NIMH. However, only one counseling psychology program [Colorado State's] is funded by NIMH as of this writing; students from other counseling psychology programs, whether APA-approved or not, are *not* eligible for NIMH-funded internships.)

Second, graduates of APA-approved programs are often considered to have met the criterion of having graduated from a professional psychology program. Thus, graduating from an approved program usually eliminates problems encountered by graduates whose programs were housed outside of psychology departments, as is often the case with counseling and school psychologists.

The third advantage is the competitive edge that a graduate of an APA-approved program has in finding a job. Employment advertisements have increasingly specified that an applicant must have a doctoral degree from an APA-approved program.

Employment advertisements have increasingly required that a candidate come from both an APA-approved training program and an APA-approved internship. The training directors of many approved programs feel that these requirements are redundant, since each training program must justify in annual reports the placement of interns in settings that are not approved by the APA. In contrast, from the perspective of the accreditation committee, those sites which a program uses which were not separately approved by APA have not been reviewed as approved sites and cannot therefore legitimately be labeled APA-approved internships. The issue is currently under review by pertinent APA committees and boards, and guidelines will probably be issued in 1980-81 on the appropriateness of requiring both forms of accreditation.

Accreditation of Training Programs by the Association of Counselor Educators and Supervisors

In 1977, the Association of Counselor Educators and Supervisors (ACES), one of the divisions of the American Personnel and Guidance Association (APGA), developed guidelines ("ACES Guidelines . . . ," 1978) for evaluating existing counselor education doctoral programs and establishing new programs. These guidelines are intended for use by state, regional, and national accrediting associations. They may be seen as the culmination of a series of developments, described by Stripling (1978), that began in 1964 with the approval by ACES and APGA of the "Standards for Counselor Education for the Preparation of Secondary School Counselors." During the next decade, other groups within the APGA developed "Guidelines for Graduate Programs in the Preparation of Student Personnel Workers in Higher Education" and "Standards for the Preparation of Elementary School Counselors." In the early 1970s, however, too much overlapping in these sets of standards became apparent, and an ACES committee was appointed to combine these standards into one document. In 1973 the "Standards for the Preparation of Counselors and Other Personnel Services Specialists" was adopted by the ACES and subsequently approved by the board of directors of the APGA. Since these guidelines primarily addressed master's-level programs, another document had to be developed for doctoral-level counseling programs.

The doctoral-level guidelines are predicated on the

assumption that the counselor education faculty is thoroughly familiar with the 1973 standards for master's-level preparation and that the master's-level program in counselor education substantially meets these standards. These "prerequisite" master's-level "Standards for Preparation of Counselors and Other Personnel Services Specialists" are readily available in the June 1977 issue of the *Personnel and Guidance Journal*. Since this set of standards can be obtained easily, it is not summarized here in detail. The major sections are comparable to those in the doctoral-level standards, which are not readily available and are therefore summarized below.

Guidelines for Doctoral Preparation in Counselor Education

Objective of the Doctoral Program in Counselor Education. The primary objective of the doctoral program in counselor education is to prepare leaders for all areas of counseling, guidance, and student services as well as counselor educators. Graduates of the program should have a strong background in the behavioral sciences. Through both didactic work and supervised experiences, they should possess strong competencies in the core areas of preparation: counseling (both individual and group), consulting, and research. Other core areas for the development of a high degree of competence might be supervision, management-administration, and facilitative or clinical teaching.

In addition to these core areas, the doctoral program should allow students to gain a depth of knowledge and skills in one or more substantive areas such as learning theory, career guidance, research, testing, or evaluation.

Curriculum-Program of Studies and Supervised Experience. A doctoral program consists of a minimum of four academic years of graduate preparation, including the entry program and a year of internship. A minimum of one academic year of full-time graduate study beyond the entry program is required.

Supervised experiences should include at least one academic year (thirty-six weeks) of full-time internship, including the one term of internship provided in the entry program.

All doctoral students should acquire competencies in statistics, research design, and other research methodology. Faculty should be involved in research that can be observed by students, and, when appropriate, students should become actively involved in this research.

Areas of specialization in which the counselor education program offers doctoral work should be clearly defined. The counselor education faculty should have the sole responsibility for selecting doctoral candidates, including the option of establishing admission criteria that are more strict than those of the graduate division of the institution. These criteria should include evidence that the applicant for the doctoral program has successfully completed entry-level preparation and experience.

The students in the doctoral program selected by the faculty should represent a variety of subcultures and subgroups within our society.

Support for the Counselor Education Program, Administrative Relationships, and Institutional Resources. Faculty members should hold doctoral degrees in areas appropriate for their programs and be recognized for their professional competencies and their commitment to the quality preparation of doctoral students.

Faculty loads should reflect an intimate professional relationship between the doctoral student and the faculty, especially those faculty who provide practicum and internship supervision. Doctoral committee chairpersons should be recognized leaders in one or more aspects of counseling, guidance, and student services and have recognized competencies in both research and writing.

In order to test and implement these guidelines, the ACES set up a pilot study in early 1979. The ACES Committee on Accreditation selected five programs for review in order to provide an in-the-field assessment of these criteria. Obviously, the development of a carefully developed accreditation process has begun ("ACES Pilot Study Begins," 1979). The expected establishment of accreditation will not only identify quality counselor education training programs but also probably affect both counselor licensing and employment opportunities. However, at these early stages in the development of both counselor licensure and the accreditation process, the specific effects cannot be determined.

Currently it is unclear whether the ACES will pursue accreditation on its own or integrate its effort with that of the APGA. In early 1979, the APGA reversed an earlier decision to make the ACES its accreditation arm. The APGA has now established a special committee on accreditation, whose recommendations regarding accreditation activities of the APGA and its constituent organizations remain to be seen ("APGA Board Reconsiders ACES Role," 1979).

Accreditation of Training Programs by the American Association for Marriage and Family Therapy

The American Association for Marriage and Family Therapy (AAMFT), formerly the American Association of Marriage and Family Counselors, has been involved in the accreditation of programs since 1949, when it worked with the National Council on Family Relations to formulate standards. In 1978, the association was formally recognized by the U.S. Department of Health, Education, and Welfare (HEW) as the national accrediting agency for the profession of marriage and family counseling. That action marked the first time that the federal government had officially acknowledged marriage and family counseling as being a distinct field of professional education and clinical training.

The specific purposes of AAMFT accreditation are (1) to improve professional marriage and family counseling education and training; (2) to establish standards for the accreditation of education and training programs that will ensure that students acquire the requisite skills, knowledge, and sense of ethics to be professionally competent; and (3) to provide an authoritative guide to programs in the field of marriage and family counseling that merit public and professional confidence and support.

As of 1979, the AAMFT had accredited seven graduate training programs in universities and six service training centers. The eligibility requirements, standards, and procedures for accreditation, summarized below, are detailed in the "Manual on Accreditation" available from the AAMFT (address in appendix).

To be considered for accreditation, a graduate training program must be located in an institution that is accredited by an appropriate regional or specialized accrediting association (see "Related Accrediting Bodies" in this chapter); the institution must offer a master's and/or doctor's degree in marriage and family counseling or a major specialization in marriage and family counseling in connection with an appropriate degree area, such as social work or marriage and family living; the institution must provide evidence of adequate support and administrative organization to ensure the stability of the program and the maintenance of adequate standards; and the program must have graduated students before being eligible for full accreditation. New or developing programs may establish a preaccreditation or candidacy status.

In order for a clinical service training program to be eligible for accreditation, the agency must meet the following four requirements: (1) It must be chartered or licensed by the appropriate state authority, if eligible; (2) trainees must have completed or be enrolled in a doctoral or master's degree program in marriage and family counseling or a closely related field, such as social work or medicine; (3) the agency must provide evidence of adequate support and the maintenance of adequate standards; and (4) the program must have been in operation for at least two full years before being eligible for full accreditation. New or developing programs may establish a preaccreditation or candidacy status if the program can reasonably be expected to attain accreditation within three years.

Eligible programs in marriage and family counseling must meet the following twenty standards, each of which is detailed in the descriptive guidelines in the manual: They must (1) have a clinical-professional structure for training and services, distinct and separate from academic, nonclinical structures; (2) have a program director who is administratively responsible for the clinical training facilities; (3) have a competent professional staff who meet the minimum professional standards for the clinical practice and supervision of marriage and family counseling; (4) have adequate facilities for providing clinical services and training; (5) have a well-defined financial policy and budget reasonably guaranteed for three years or longer; (6) have accepted personnel practices for teaching, clinical service, and administrative personnel; (7) provide for interpretation of services to the community; (8) have professionally qualified marriage and family counselors, at least some of whom are members of the AAMFT; (9) have supervisors with training experience and demonstrated ability in teaching and supervising trainees or staff in the practice of marriage and family counseling, at least some of whom are able to meet the requirements for designation as "approved supervisors" by the AAMFT; (10) have experienced personnel from appropriate behavioral science and clinical fields who are available to the staff and trainees as needed for didactic, supervisory, or consultative purposes; (11) provide trainees with a reasonable number of and variety of cases, such as premarriage counseling, marriage counseling, divorce and remarriage counseling, and family therapy and group couples counseling; (12) have systematic, confidential record keeping of the type that is essential for teaching marriage and family counseling and for evaluating the service provided; (13) maintain confidentiality of all clinical records and interviews; (14) have a clearly stated policy concerning the establishment and collection of fees; (15) require that trainees be enrolled in a doctoral or master's program in marriage and family, psychology, sociology, or a closely related field, or, if enrolled as a special student, have completed a degree at an appropriately accredited graduate school or professional school and have the personal qualifications and readiness for clinical training; (16) expose students to important areas of theoretical competency, including personality theory, psychopathology, human sexuality, marriage and family studies, marriage counseling, and family therapy; (17) provide practice in marriage and family counseling in a training year; (18) provide supervision that must involve face-to-face meetings with the supervisor, be sustained and intense, usually once a week over a period of one or more years, focus on the raw material from the supervisee's current clinical work, and be both clearly distinguishable from psychotherapy and intended to serve professional goals; (19) recognize the role and value of personal psychotherapy and encourage trainees to secure such assistance for their personal and professional development; and (20) evaluate the trainee's clinical competence and fitness for practice.

The standards for clinical service training programs are similar, with minor changes in wording to reflect the differences in settings.

The implications of AAMFT accreditation are similar to those discussed in the general introduction to this chapter. Graduating from an accredited training program makes it easier to obtain training from an accredited clinical service training program, and applicants for positions as marriage and family therapists are sometimes required to have received training in an accredited program or institute.

After December 31, 1983, accreditation will affect eligibility as a clinical member of the AAMFT. Applicants will be required to have a master's or doctoral degree in marriage and family therapy from an accredited institution or a master's or doctoral degree in an allied mental health profession whose curriculum fully meets the course of study required for eligibility (see Chapter Eight).

Accreditation of Training Programs by the Council on Rehabilitation Education

The Council on Rehabilitation Education (CORE) was formed in 1971 with the basic purpose of promoting the effective delivery of rehabilitation services by reviewing and improving master's-level rehabilitation counselor education programs. The council is made up of two representatives each from five professional rehabilitation organizations: the American Rehabilitation Counseling Association, the National Council on Rehabilitation Education, the Council of State Administrators of Vocational Rehabilitation, the Association of Rehabilitation Facilities, and the National Rehabilitation Counseling Association.

In its early years, the council, with the support of the Rehabilitation Service Administration of the U.S. Department of Health, Education, and Welfare, developed an evaluation procedure based primarily on assessing the performance of graduates. The council revised and revalidated its standards in 1977 and 1978. Fifty-six master's-level programs in rehabilitation counseling are currently accredited ("Rehabilitation Programs Now Accredited," 1979). The evaluations of these programs, as well as the development and implementation of standards, is a responsibility of the Commission on Standards and Accreditation. This commission is composed of five CORE and five non-CORE members, each nominated by one of the five participating organizations, plus five at-large members selected from the general public, especially to represent minorities, consumers, and disciplines and agencies closely related to rehabilitation counseling.

Three categories of accreditation are offered, each with separate criteria for eligibility. Candidacy for accreditation is a status accorded to programs in the early stages of development up to the point of graduating their first students. Preliminary accreditation is granted to programs that have been fully operational for one year but do not have enough graduates to allow objective assessment of their graduates' performance. Accreditation is granted to programs that have been fully operational long enough for the professional performance of at least thirty graduates to be objectively assessed. Of all the educational program accreditation procedures for the professions of psychology and counseling, only CORE includes the assessment of graduates' performance.

In order to be eligible for any of these categories of accreditation, the educational institution must be accredited by the appropriate regional accreditation body, offer other graduate degrees in addition to rehabilitation education, and have the equivalent of one full-time faculty position assigned to the program.

Standards for Rehabilitation Counselor Education Programs. The first of six sections on standards specifies that there shall be a written statement of the program's mission and objectives, a written rationale and documentation of the need for the program, evidence of the expression of the program's missions and objective accomplishments to its public, systematic procedures for the periodic review and revision of the program's objectives, and written evidence of the program's commitment to the development of practitioners, educators, and researchers. The program shall provide professional contributions to the community that are consistent with its mission and have mechanisms to assess fulfillment of its mission.

A second section specifies the personnel and fiscal support that are necessary, as well as the clerical staff, instructional quarters, and instructional media required. The campus and its facilities must also be accessible to and usable by the disabled (Council on Rehabilitation Education, Inc., 1978).

Full-time graduate study for two academic years is required. Twenty-six content areas are required to provide the essential knowledge, skills, and attitudes necessary to function effectively as a professional rehabilitation counselor. Some of these areas are planning client vocational rehabilitation services, theories and practices of assessment and evaluation, counseling theories and practices, environmental impact on aspects of disability, rehabilitation research literature, and legal and ethical issues in the practice of rehabilitation counseling. Beyond formal course work, supervised clinical experience of at least 600 hours in accredited rehabilitation-agency settings under the supervision of certified rehabilitation counselors is required.

The faculty must be of adequate size and have appropriate qualifications for carrying out the program's mission, evidence of affirmative action for disabled, include nonwhite and female members, and evidence that the faculty engage in placement activities for students completing the program.

Standards regarding students require evidence of affirmative action for disabled and nonwhite students, the existence of a student financial assistance plan, and evidence that the program provides the guidance and opportunities necessary to assure the graduation of qualified students. The students must be evaluated in twenty-one different areas such as academic knowledge and interaction with consumers.

The final section of standards concerns the assessment of a program's graduates. In addition to helping graduates obtain appropriate employment, the program is required to record and assess data in six areas of graduate students' performance, for example, percentage of graduates employed in public or private agencies for the handicapped and the contribution of graduates to the profession of vocational rehabilitation. There must also be evidence that the graduates are prepared to perform rehabilitation counseling tasks in eight different areas: (1) interpretation of medical, educational, social, and vocational evaluation for individual clients; (2) rehabilitation planning and case management for individual clients; (3) career and vocational counseling for individual clients; (4) personal and social counseling for individual clients; (5) job development and placement for individual clients; (6) use of community resources; (7) recording and reporting for individual clients; and (8) professional participation and development.

The manual (Council on Rehabilitation Education, Inc., 1978) describes all of these standards in detail as well as elaborating on application, evaluation, appeals, reapplication, and site visit procedures.

International Association of Counseling Services

The International Association of Counseling Services (IACS) accredits agencies that provide counseling services. In contrast to the accreditation agencies just reviewed, which evaluate either training programs or internship programs, IACS does not accredit academic programs. While many IACS-accredited agencies include internship training programs, IACS accreditation relates to the service functions of the agency. Accreditation by the IACS serves two very important roles: maintaining and enhancing standards within counseling agencies and protecting the counseling clientele.

The IACS, a separate corporation loosely affiliated with the APGA, is a voluntary accreditation organization. A service agency applies to the IACS; if it appears to meet accreditation criteria on its application, an IACS site visitation team goes to the agency and then reports its findings and recommendations to an accrediting board. The appropriate accrediting board makes the final determination. There are three such accrediting boards within the organization, each having its own criteria and relating to services delivered within different settings. One board deals with public and private agencies, ranging from private-practice counseling agencies to the counseling services within, for example, a state employment agency. A second board evaluates counseling services that are units of colleges or universities, while a third pertains to counseling within community, technical, and junior colleges. The IACS is governed by a board of directors representing a cross section of these three domains.

The criteria for developing an accredited service in a college and counseling center are readily available in the June 1971 *American Psychologist* (vol. 26, no. 6, pp. 585-589). Consequently, only the topical areas of the guidelines are summarized here.

The guidelines define the role of counseling as providing both developmental and remedial services and specify the need to make the availability of its services well known to students and other members of the university or college community. Staff members are expected to provide advisory and consultative services to the faculty, to provide training for graduate students as appropriate, and to engage in research to determine the effectiveness of its services. Guidelines on personnel outline desired qualifications, professional contributions, continuing professional development, compensation, work load, and supporting staff. Other sections specify referral procedures and physical facilities that should be available. The criteria for community, junior, and technical college counseling centers and for public and private counseling services cover similar areas with appropriate changes made for the different settings.

While the IACS is a relatively young organization, incorporated in 1972, it was an extension of an earlier organization, the American Board on Counseling Services, which had been in existence for many years. In 1979, IACS included in its annual directory approximately 260 accredited agencies and is currently engaged in a campaign to attract more applicants. Apart from its accrediting function, the IACS publishes both an annual directory, which may be found in many libraries and referral services, and a member newsletter. The IACS also maintains an information clearinghouse that places a member who needs information or expertise in a particular professional area in contact with other member agencies that can supply it.

Because IACS members are agencies rather than individuals, the IACS relates only tangentially to the individual counselor or psychologist. However, as part of the accreditation process, the professional qualifications of individual staff members and directors are scrutinized; consequently, persons desiring such positions must meet the IACS specifications. For the college and university sector, the counseling director must have an earned doctorate in counseling psychology, clinical psychology, or counseling and be eligible for certification or licensure. Certification as an elementary or secondary school counselor will not suffice. A waiver of the licensure or certification requirement can be granted in special situations upon formal application. At the present time, these licensure and certification requirements for the director of an accredited college or university counseling center have been interpreted as relating to psychologists. However, should more licensure or certification laws for counselors be passed similar to the generic counselor licensure acts in Virginia, Arkansas, and Alabama, the IACS guidelines would, in their current form, presumably accept such licensure for meeting the IACS licensure stipulation.

The advantages of this type of credentialing are the same as the general advantages of institutional accreditation noted at the beginning of this chapter.

Agencies frequently face two problems in the IACS accreditation process. First, the service director in a university or college service agency often does not hold a doctoral degree in psychology or higher education, thereby making the institution ineligible for IACS accreditation. Second, many agencies, for a variety of administrative reasons as well as individual reasons, do not maintain the high degree of confidentiality of records that the IACS requires. In some academic settings, administrators and faculty see it as their duty to review students' counseling records. Agencies that do not have administrative support for the confidentiality of records as defined by the IACS are not eligible for IACS accreditation.

Private and Governmental Authorizations for Accreditation

Both private and governmental agencies grant the authority to accredit educational programs. As educational settings become increasingly subject to accreditation reviews, those agencies become more and more important in determining how accreditation is conducted. The typical counselor or psychologist does not have direct interactions with these organizations. However, most of the accrediting groups described thus far do have such interactions; moreover, the nature of their policies and procedures is in part dictated by two organizations: the Council of Post Secondary Accreditation (COPA) and the Division of Eligibility and Evaluation of the U.S. Office of Education.

COPA is a nonprofit, nongovernmental organization whose major purpose is to support, coordinate, and improve all nongovernmental accrediting activities conducted at the postsecondary educational level in the United States. It encompasses fifty-two accrediting bodies, which provide institutional and/or programmatic accreditation in 4,000 institutions of postsecondary education.

COPA was created in 1975 as an amalgamation of the Federation of Regional Accreditation Commissions of Higher Education (FRACHE) and the National Commission on Accrediting. FRACHE had been composed of the six regional accrediting associations: the Middle States Association of Colleges and Schools, the New England Association of Colleges and Schools, the North Central Association of Colleges and Schools, the Northwest Association of Colleges and Schools, the Southern Association of Colleges and Schools, and the Western Association of Colleges and Schools. The National Commission on Accrediting, founded in 1949, as was FRACHE, had had the responsibility to review, recognize by listing, and continue to monitor the activities of specialized programmatic bodies.

COPA now recognizes thirty-nine specialized accrediting groups that accredit over 3,600 programs. Other accrediting bodies that are members of COPA are related to particular types of institutions, for example, Bible colleges.

COPA is administered by a board of thirty-six persons representing all types of institutions, accrediting bodies, and the general public. In 1978 the board identified five major priorities: dealing with the problems associated with proliferation and specialization in accreditation; evaluating educational quality; coping with the role of government in accreditation; developing a national education information program on accreditation; and selecting, training, and evaluating volunteers in accreditation. COPA has also established procedures for receiving complaints that institutions or programs wish to make against its recognized accrediting bodies; however, COPA is not a clearinghouse for individual consumer complaints against institutions or programs of study. More extensive information on COPA, its board members, and contact persons for all the regional and programmatic accrediting groups may be obtained by writing to COPA (address in appendix) and requesting their 1978 booklet "COPA: The Balance Wheel for Accreditation." Detailed information on how to apply for recognition as an accrediting agency and how to make complaints against a recognized accrediting body may be found in their 1975 (and still current) publication "Provisions and Procedures for Becoming Recognized as an Accrediting Agency for Postsecondary Educational Institutions or Programs."

The Division of Eligibility and Agency Evaluation of the U.S. Office of Education is more commonly, if erroneously, referred to as the HEW Office of Accrediting. This division was established in 1968 by the commissioner of education to determine eligibility for federal assistance under certain legislation. The division is required to publish a list of nationally recognized accrediting associations judged to be reliable authorities on the quality of training offered by educational institutions and programs. The primary work of this division is carried out by the Advisory Committee on Accreditation and Institutional Eligibility, a committee composed of fifteen persons who are appointed to three-year terms by the Secretary of Health, Education, and Welfare and who come from various segments of the secondary and postsecondary education community, including the students, state departments of education, professional associations, and the general public. Of the fifteen major functions of the committee, the two that are most pertinent to counselors and psychologists are its obligation to develop and recommend criteria and procedures for the recognition and designation of accrediting agencies and associations and its obligation to review and recommend for designation by the Commissioner of Education those accrediting agencies and associations that meet the established criteria. Further details on the division, its procedures for recognition, and its constituent members and board members may be obtained by requesting the booklet "Nationally Recognized Accrediting Agencies and Associations" from the Division of Eligibility and Agency Evaluation in the HEW Office of Education (address in appendix).

While this division was originally set up to determine eligibility for assistance under legislation requiring accreditation, the status accompanying such recognition has encouraged many specialized accrediting agencies to seek recognition from the division. Such recognition is then interpreted as evidence of distinctive professional stature; this stature is then used to support the development of various types of licensing and credentialing. An unintentional implication of such recognition, then, is an increasing number of petitions from ever more narrowly defined professions.

Both COPA and HEW are concerned with this proliferation, especially because of the numerous site visits that it spawns, which are immensely costly in terms of both time and money. COPA suggests that new groups seeking the authorization to accredit first consider four alternatives: (1) developing educational and consultation services in lieu of accreditation, (2) working informally with existing accrediting bodies, (3) becoming part of an existing accrediting body, and (4) joining existing or new accrediting bodies to create a larger umbrella organization. Obviously, COPA is attempting to discourage the development of new accreditation groups.

Additionally, COPA is preparing a task force that will encourage accrediting bodies to cooperate in areas such as terminology, common site visits, coordinated self-study, and the design of annual report forms to provide more information to COPA, institutions, and the agencies themselves ("Cooperation to Be Theme of Conference," 1978). In the coming years, increasing pressure will be placed on accrediting groups to make joint site visits, especially where similar groups have jurisdiction over the same programs, such as the National Council for Accreditation of Teacher Education and the ACES, which will soon accredit counselor education programs. Pilot accreditations are underway at six programs now. If too many problems emerge, it may be years before a full accreditation system is operational.

Over the next few years, as the HEW Division of Eligibility and Agency Evaluation and COPA work together and with their various subordinate groups, the current operations of the accrediting agencies reviewed in this chapter will likely be challenged and in some cases changed.

Related Accrediting Bodies

Three other commissions accredit training programs or services in which psychologists and counselors work, even though their accreditation does not specifically apply to the psychology or counseling component. These commissions are mentioned here to indicate how they affect the work of psychologists and counselors. Details on their criteria and procedures are not provided because of their much broader scope.

Regional Accreditation of Educational Institutions. Six regional accrediting associations in the United States review and accredit entire educational institutions. (Individual program accreditation is granted only by specialized accrediting bodies; however, most specialized program accreditation requires that the housing institution be regionally accredited.)

While the six accrediting bodies differ somewhat, the accrediting process of each basically begins with an institution's self-assessment of the effectiveness of its program in light of its publicly stated purposes and objectives. This self-study should include the opinions of students, faculty, trustees, administrators, alumni, and perhaps persons from the local community. The self-study and background material is sent to an evaluation team, which then visits the campus. The site-visiting team is made up of faculty members and administrators as well as certain specialists, according to the nature of the institution. Site visitors appraise the institution's own efforts to assess its strengths and weaknesses. "Once an evaluation team completes its report and the institution or program reviews it for factual accuracy, the report goes to a designated reviewing body along with the original self-study report and any further response the institution makes to the analysis and judgments óf the visiting team. The accrediting bodies then consider the evidence and take appropriate action, with adequate provisions for appeal in accordance with due process" (American Council on Education, 1979). While institutions are ordinarily reviewed every ten years, an institution may be asked for an earlier review if it undergoes substantial change, such as offering new levels of degrees.

Since institutions can be fully accredited only after having established a stable, productive program with graduates, the status "candidate for accreditation" is provided. This particular category is of importance to consumers, since it indicates that the institution is moving toward becoming fully accredited. "The institution must provide evidence of sound planning, the resources to implement these plans and appear to have the potential for attaining its goals within a reasonable time" (American Council on Education, 1979). The eight characteristics that qualify an institution to apply as a candidate for accreditation are fully outlined in the annual publication *Accredited Institutions of Postsecondary Education*.

It is important to note that institutions of postsecondary education can exist for decades without regional accreditation. Each state has separate requirements that govern the establishment of educational institutions. "Diploma mills," that is, schools that grant diplomas with little or no real evidence of instruction, may be operating entirely according to state law.

Such programs usually lack regional accreditation, and for this reason accrediting bodies increasingly specify that training must take place in regionally accredited institutions.

Equally important, however, is that new schools must exist for several years before applying for regional accreditation. Thus, one cannot assume that a regionally unaccredited school, especially if it is new, is a diploma mill. The careful consumer will determine whether a new school is at least moving toward candidate status.

National Council for the Accreditation of Teacher Education. The National Council for the Accreditation of Teacher Education (NCATE) is authorized to accredit college and university programs that prepare teachers and other professional school personnel at the elementary and secondary levels and has increasingly interacted with the accreditation activities of the APA and the APGA (the former because of the school psychology, the latter because of counselor education). This has created some problems over which agency should accredit certain programs. In particular, the question has arisen as to whether the NCATE or the APA should accredit school psychology programs. Currently the APA approves only doctoral-level school psychology programs. As a result, master's-level school psychologists favor accreditation by NCATE, which accredits master's-level programs. A similar controversy is emerging as the ACES develops its accreditation policies for counselor education programs, which typically train personnel for elementary and secondary schools. The issue has been exacerbated because universities have been applying increasing pressure recently to restrict the amount of independent accrediting operations, since much time is required to prepare for the multiple site visits from the many different agencies. In early 1979 the APGA became an associate member of the National Council of the NCATE so that it could participate in NCATE debates and, it hopes, preclude jurisdictional disputes such as that between the APA and the NCATE.

Joint Commission on Accreditation of Hospitals. Psychologists or counselors working in hospital settings are often subject to the requirements of the Joint Commission on Accreditation of Hospitals (JCAH). Of the agencies accrediting hospitals in the United States, the JCAH is by far the largest, certifying approximately 70 percent of the almost 7,500 hospitals in the country. The JCAH was founded in 1913 by the American College of Surgeons (ACS) to improve hospital conditions and primary hospital care for patients. Since that time it has developed accreditation standards for hospitals and applied them in on-site hospital inspections. This effort was solely that of the ACS until 1950, when it was joined by several other medical groups—the American College of Physicians (ACP), the American Hospital Association (AHA), the American Medical Association (AMA) and, until 1959, the Canadian Medical Association. This amalgamation, finalized in 1951, is governed by a board of commissioners consisting of seven members from both the AMA and the AHA and three from both the ACP and the ACS.

The first of four accreditation councils was established in 1969, the Accreditation Council for Services for the Mentally Retarded and Other Developmentally Disabled Persons. The other three formed were the Accreditation Council for Long-Term Care Facilities (1971), the Accreditation Council for Psychiatric Facilities (1970), and the Accreditation Council for Ambulatory Health Care (1975). Like the JCAH itself, seats on these councils are apportioned by the joint commission among appropriate member groups (like the APA). Formal input from nonphysician organizations and associations comes only from the twenty-four different member groups of the four accreditation councils.

The JCAH explicitly maintains its dominance by physicians, as expressed in the JCAH-government relations "position paper": "JCAH owes its first allegiance and responsibilities to those health professions and institutions which have created it and give it sustenance" (JCAH joint conference committee meeting minutes, July 12, 1975). The JCAH standards, which are important and wide reaching, are incorporated in such legislation as Medicaid, Medicare, and the Civilian Health and Medical Program of the Uniformed Services (CHAMPUS). These standards exclude licensed or certified psychologists and counselors from engaging in independent practice within a hospital setting. "None of the state statutes that license and certify psychologists requires supervision of a physician, none limit the settings in which psychologists may practice and none prohibit them from treating inpatients. As a direct result of restrictive JCAH policies, however, psychologists are barred from independent practice in inpatient facilities" (O'Keefe and McCullough, 1979, p. 610). The implications for psychologists of JCAH standards for psychiatric facilities are discussed in Dörken and Morrison (1976), and for community mental health service programs in Fiester (1978).

At present two movements relating to JCAH are of interest to psychologists. First, in 1976 the Association for the Advancement of Psychology, the public advocacy arm of the APA, in conjunction with the Federal Trade Commission, initiated a formal complaint concerning the medical profession's dominance of treatment planning and service in mental health treatment, essentially asking for psychological services for inpatients to be independent of medical supervision. By 1979 this issue had not been resolved. Second, JCAH, in the process of centralizing its powers in its board of commissioners, replaced the four accreditation councils in June 1979 with "Professional and Technical Advisory Committees" that had no policy-making roles or accreditation responsibilities. After this action, "three of the five member organizations of the Accreditation Council for Ambulatory Health Care . . . withdrew from JCAH. Together with three organizations not affiliated with JCAH, they formed the independent Accreditation Association for Ambulatory Health Care (AAAHC). It remains to be seen whether AAAHC can compete with JCAH, which has attained a quasi-governmental status, at least in the field of hospital accreditation" (O'Keefe and McCullough, 1979, p. 610).

Standards for Providers of Psychological Services

In 1974 the APA adopted a set of standards as a means of self-regulation to protect the public interest. "The intent of these standards is to improve the quality, effectiveness, and accessibility of psychological services to all who require them"

(American Psychological Association, 1977b). Although the standards are not a type of accreditation, they are one of the bases on which agency and individual service providers are evaluated by peer review organizations. Consequently, service-providing psychologists must expect to meet these standards in order to remain in good standing in the profession.

These standards were developed during the early 1970s, when the APA Board of Professional Affairs became aware of its responsibility to determine standards for psychological practice in the broad range of human service settings. Without such self-regulation, psychologists ran the risk of courts or other bodies outside the profession setting minimum standards. The APA standards set the *minimum* acceptable levels of quality as well as the minimum levels of psychologists' training for all psychological services, both private and public. This was a significant change from the prior APA position, which favored exclusions in state legislation for persons providing psychological services under governmental or other institutional auspices. "This circumstance tends to afford greater protection under the law for those receiving privately delivered psychological services; on the other hand, those receiving privately delivered psychological services currently lack many of the safeguards that are available in governmental settings; these include peer review, consultation, record review, staff supervision" (American Psychological Association, 1977b, p. 3).

While copies of the standards are available without charge to all APA members, we find that fellow professionals are relatively unaware of them as compared with ethical standards. Consequently, the standards and critical definitions are printed in their entirety here. The explanatory footnotes and interpretations are not included and are available from the APA by requesting a free copy of *Standards for Providers of Psychological Services.*

Providers of psychological services refers to the following persons: A. Professional psychologists. Professional psychologists have a doctoral degree from a regionally accredited university or professional school in a program that is primarily psychological and appropriate training and experience in the area of service offered. B. All other persons who offer psychological services under the supervision of a professional psychologist.

Psychological Services refers to one or more of the following: A. Evaluation, diagnosis, and assessment of the functioning of individuals and groups in a variety of settings and activities. B. Interventions to facilitate the functioning of individuals and groups. Such interventions may include psychological counseling, psychotherapy, and process consultation. C. Consultation relating to A and B above. D. Program development services in the area of A, B, and C above. E. Supervision of psychological services.

A psychological service unit is the functional unit through which psychological services are provided.

User includes: A. Direct users or recipients of psychological services. B. Public and private institutions, facilities, or organizations receiving psychological services. C. Third-party purchasers—those who pay for the delivery of services but who are not the recipients of services.

Sanctioners refers to those users and nonusers who have a legitimate concern with the accessibility, timeliness, efficacy, and standards of quality attending to provision of psychological services. In addition to the users, sanctioners may include members of the user's family, the court, the probation officer, the school administrator, the employer, the union representative, the facility director, and so on. Another class of sanctioners is represented by various governmental, peer review, and accreditation bodies concerned with the assurance of quality.

1. Providers:

   1.1 Each psychological service unit offering psychological services shall have available at least one professional psychologist and as many more professional psychologists as are necessary to assure the quality of services offered.

   1.2 Providers of psychological services who do not meet the requirements for the professional psychologist shall be supervised by a professional psychologist who shall assume professional responsibility and accountability for the services provided. The level and extent of supervision may vary from task to task so long as the supervising psychologist retains a sufficiently close supervisory relationship to meet this standard.

1.3 Wherever a psychological service unit exists, a professional psychologist shall be responsible for planning, directing, and reviewing the provision of psychological services.

1.4 When functioning as part of an organizational setting, professional psychologists shall bring their background and skills to bear whenever appropriate upon the goals of the organization by participating in the planning and development of overall services.

1.5 Psychologists shall maintain current knowledge of scientific and professional developments that are directly related to the services they render.

1.6 Psychologists shall limit their practice to their demonstrated areas of professional competence.

1.7 Psychologists who wish to change their service specialty or to add an additional area of applied specialization must meet the same requirements with respect to subject matter and professional skills that apply to doctoral training in the new specialty.

2. Programs:

2.1 Composition and organization of a psychological service unit:

2.1.1. The composition and programs of a psychological service unit shall be responsive to the needs of the persons or settings served.

2.1.2. A description of the organization of the psychological service unit and its lines of responsibility and accountability for the delivery of psychological services shall be available in written form to staff of the unit and to users and sanctioners upon request.

2.1.3. A psychological service unit shall include sufficient numbers of professional and support personnel to achieve its goals, objectives, and purposes.

2.2 Policies:

2.2.1. When the psychological service unit is composed of more than one person wherein a supervisory relationship exists or is a component of a larger organization, a written statement of its objectives and scope of services shall be developed and maintained.

2.2.2. All providers within a psychological service unit shall support the legal and civil rights of the user.

2.2.3. All providers within a psychological service unit shall be familiar with and adhere to the American Psychological Association's Ethical Standards of Psychologists, Psychology as a Profession, Standards for Educational and Psychological Tests, and other official policy statements relevant to standards for professional services issued by the Association.

2.2.4. All providers within a psychological service unit shall conform to relevant statutes established by federal, state, and local government.

2.2.5. All providers within a psychological service unit shall, where appropriate, inform themselves about and use the network of human services in their communities in order to link users with relevant services and resources.

2.2.6. In the delivery of psychological services, the providers shall maintain a continuing cooperative relationship with colleagues and co-workers whenever in the best interest of the user.

2.3 Procedures:

2.3.1. Where appropriate, each psychological service unit shall be guided by a set of procedural guidelines for the delivery of psychological services. If appropriate to the setting, these guidelines shall be in written form.

2.3.2. Providers shall develop a plan appropriate to the provider's professional strategy of practice and to the problems presented by the user.

2.3.3. There shall be a mutually acceptable understanding between the provider and user or responsible agent regarding the delivery of service.

2.3.4. Accurate, current, and pertinent documentation shall be made of essential psychological services provided.

2.3.5. Providers of psychological services shall establish a system to protect confidentiality of their records.

3. Accountability:

3.1 Psychologists' professional activity shall be primarily guided by the principle of promoting human welfare.

3.2 Psychologists shall pursue their activities as members of an independent, autonomous profession.

3.3 There shall be periodic, systematic, and effective evaluations of psychological services.

3.4 Psychologists are accountable for all aspects of the services they provide and shall be responsive to those concerned with these services.

4. Environment: Providers of psychological services shall promote the development in the service setting of a physical, organizational, and social environment that facilitates optimal human functioning [American Psychological Association, 1977b, pp. 4-11].

Implications and Issues. The most significant standard for psychologists is, of course, the requirement that an unsupervised practitioner hold a doctoral degree. This step was consistent with earlier positions taken by the APA, as discussed in earlier chapters. In several states requiring only the master's degree for independent practice, licensed practitioners are not in accord with this APA minimum standard.

In fact, a careful, narrowly interpreted reading of the standards makes clear that many psychological service settings are not in full accord with APA standards. Most often violated are standards 1.3 (in many community mental health centers, no psychologist is responsible for planning, directing, or reviewing the provisions of psychological services), 2.1.2. (the majority of psychological services outside of large institutional settings do not have written organizational plans), and 3.3 (all too few agencies conduct regular, systematic evaluations of their psychological services).

Counselors who are not psychologists have expressed concern (*Licensure Committee Action Packet,* 1979) that these standards could significantly affect the profession of counseling. A strict interpretation could require counselors to be supervised by psychologists simply to fulfill their well-established roles in education and community service centers. Counselors, then, feel that many of the same issues created by licensing could be exacerbated by the standards.

Enforcing these standards at this point remains the responsibility of users and sanctioners, who must bring to the attention of administrators and accreditation agencies those persons who are not in compliance. Many states have developed professional standards review committees to provide a grievance procedure for complainants.

Specialty Standards. Another emerging issue concerns the development of specialty (for example, counseling, clinical, school, and so on) standards by the APA. Specialty standards are a direct outgrowth of the generic standards as noted in section 1.6 (see page 148). They are seen as supplements to generic standards. Initially these standards were intended to clarify the types of training and conditions required to offer services in each of these specialties. Industrial-organizational psychologists provided much of the impetus for developing these specialty standards, because they found the 1974 generic standards to be more pertinent to the provision of mental health services than the provision of consultation and organizational development services. From 1976 to 1979, the APA Committee on Standards for Providers of Psychological Services prepared drafts of specialty standards. The initial drafts described training, types of services, and organizational and administrative issues related to each specialty. Reviews of these drafts by various boards and committees of the APA as well as by training program and internship directors expressed great concern about the detail of training standards in each of the four specialties. Training directors in the specialties felt that the distinctions drawn did not well describe the full range of professional abilities in each specialty; moreover, detailing specialty training restricted the possibilities for innovation. Revised drafts thus removed all specifications regarding training. Additionally, responding to legal advice, the remaining standards were changed from a mandatory *shall* to an advisory *should*. In early 1980 these altered drafts were adopted as guidelines, rather than standards, by the APA Council of Representatives.

Some psychologists believe that the remaining guidelines could excessively compartmentalize functions of psychologists in a variety of settings, limit the possibilities for innovation, and greatly increase the amount of administrative bureaucracy needed in settings that employ psychologists from several specialties. Many have questioned the need for specialty standards if the existing ethical standard that psychologists shall limit their practice to demonstrated areas of professional competence is closely followed.

Many psychologists also worry that specialty standards will encourage the development of specialty licensing, which could fragment already fragile alliances of psychology specialties. As discussed in the section on specialty licensing in Chapter Four, third-party payers, that is, insurance payers, in their effort to restrict as much as possible the number of people who should be reimbursed, have already utilized the supposedly generic "clinical psychologist" title for reimbursement. If licensing should occur for the most common specialties, that is, clinical, school, counseling, and industrial-organizational psychology, these types of psychologists could experience new difficulties in being reimbursed for mental health services they now perform.

In addition, while the APA now recognizes four specialties, many other groups have petitions to identify their area as a specialty, including psychoanalytic psychology and behavior modification. As new specialties are designated, will new sets of guidelines have to be developed for each?

Professional Standards Review Committees

Professional standards review committees (PSRCs) have developed fairly recently, since the concept has only recently been applied to patients under mental health care. Professional standards review organizations (PSROs) have existed for a longer time, as they were originally mandated by federal regulations to cover medical patients. A PSRO typically reviews hospital services offered in a designated geographic area. Since membership in PSROs has been legally restricted to physicians, psychologists have shown considerable interest in developing their own standards and review committees so that they could have exclusive review of their own cases. As counselors become licensed in more states, *and* if they become eligible for insurance payments, similar developments may arise.

A PSRC is intended to augment state licensure and certification and state insurance codes so that a profession can set up its own responsible, effective grievance procedure to investigate complaints about services or fees.

In usual practice, consumers or third-party payers ask a state PSRC to render opinions as to whether a particular practice or procedure is usual, customary, or reasonable (with these three terms having very precise definitions). The PSRC attempts to determine (1) whether a particular service was really needed by the client, (2) whether the manner of providing the services met professionally recognized standards, (3) whether another approach or facility might have been preferable, and (4) whether the fees charged were appropriate. While the PSRC is usually set up by the state psychological association, it may review cases relating to nonmembers, since it relates to the profession within the state and not just to the state association.

Once the PSRC has received a formal request, the committee will process the case, maintaining the client's right to privacy, interview the psychologist involved if appropriate (or at least obtain written material from the psychologist), and then render a judgment after a full and very confidential deliberation. A written report of this judgment is sent to the psychologist, the complainant, and the client if the client has been involved in the processing of the case. The party initiating the case for review will presumably accept the PSRC's disposition of the case, although well-established PSRCs have appeal procedures.

In addition to the state PSRC committees, the APA has collaborated with CHAMPUS to provide a national peer review manual that defines the standards of care administered by psychologists to CHAMPUS patients (Claiborn and Stricker, 1979). The most recent information on the development and implementation of this system may be obtained by requesting a copy of "Update," a periodic publication of the APA/ CHAMPUS Project, housed in the APA (address in appendix).

Two points should be noted about PSRCs. First, a PSRC does not review alleged ethical violations, which should be referred to the profession's state or national ethics committee and/or to the state's statutory board or commission. Second, a PSRC is not a policing agency that looks for possible violations of the state certification or licensure law; such violations should be referred to the state statutory board or commission.

A state PSRC must be well publicized to be effective. The state association has the responsibility of informing professionals, the public at large, and third-party payers of a PSRC's existence and functions. Equally important, well-informed and professionally responsible practitioners will not only learn about their local PSRC but also involve themselves in state associations so that they can participate in the formulation of policies that govern PSRCs and in other actions that increase the profession's responsiveness to its constituencies.

Listings Often Misconstrued as Credentials

Various directories are issued that list programs in psychology and/or counseling. *Graduate Study in Psychology,* published annually by the APA, lists hundreds of master's and doctoral degree programs in psychology and related areas. Periodically a *Counselor Education Directory* is published (Hollis and Wantz, 1977). Both publications provide information based on the self-reports of programs and thereby indicate the intentions of the listed schools. However, readers should note that the material is not validated by external review. Thus, these listings should not be used as evidence that either profession has approved of a listed program. Similarly, the APA has stated that membership in the organization is in no way to be construed as "evidence of qualification" (American Psychological Association, 1977a, p. 3).

8

Other Forms of Professional Credentials

This chapter focuses on voluntary types of credentialing for individuals. The types of credentialing reviewed here are independent of state or federal legislation; that is, they are nonstatutory credentialing. For psychologists and counselors, six forms of such credentialing are pertinent; however, specialized training is needed within psychology or counseling to qualify for any of them. The credentials reviewed are the diploma from the American Board of Professional Psychology (ABPP), listing in the National Register for Health Service Providers in Psychology, certification by the National Board of Certified Mental Health Counselors, clinical membership in the American Association for Marriage and Family Therapists (AAMFT), certification from the American Association of Sex Educators and Counselors (AASEC), and certification from the Commission on Rehabilitation Counselor Certification.

156

Each of these forms of credentialing examines credentials and/or competence more closely than do major professional interest organizations such as the American Psychological Association (APA) and the American Personnel and Guidance Association (APGA). For the first two types of credentialing reviewed, one must be a doctoral-level psychologist. For the other four, psychologists, counselors, and a broad array of mental health professionals at either the master's or doctoral level may be eligible provided training requirements are met.

The major benefit of these forms of credentialing, besides having a diploma to post on the office wall, is access to certain kinds of positions and types of reimbursement for services that are difficult, if not impossible, to attain without such credentials. Each of these forms of credentialing has evolved with distinct purposes and specific benefits, and each poses distinct problems for counselors and psychologists.

It is important to note that membership in professional organizations such as the APA, the APGA, or any of their divisions does not represent a form of credentialing. Membership in these organizations represents professional interest rather than a thorough evaluation of training or experience. For example, many members of the APA and the APGA would not qualify for certification or licensing in any state as a psychologist or counselor.

American Board of Professional Psychology

The American Board of Professional Psychology, Inc., originally incorporated as the American Board of Examiners in Professional Psychology, was established in 1947 in order to (1) grant, issue, and control the use of its diploma of special competence in fields of professional psychology and (2) to arrange, conduct, and control investigations and examinations to determine the qualifications of individuals who make voluntary application for such diplomas.

The Board now awards diplomas in four professional specialties: Clinical Psychology, Counseling

Psychology, Industrial and Organizational Psychology, and School Psychology.

The Board encourages the pursuit of excellence via its program of certification at an advanced professional level. The ABPP diploma signifies, to the public and to the profession, the highest recognition of competence as judged by one's professional peers [American Board of Professional Psychology, 1978, p. 1].

To apply for the ABPP diploma, as of July 1, 1980, a doctoral degree from an APA-approved program or a program clearly labeled as part of a psychology department is required. In either case, the program completed by the graduate must satisfy the criteria developed at the 1977 Education and Credentialing Conference (see Chapter Three) and have had one or more faculty members or internship supervisors with evidence of distinction, such as fellow status in the APA or ABPP diplomate status. Additionally, clinical, counseling, and school psychologist applicants must have completed an internship of 1,800 hours in no more than two years in a health service setting or in another organized, appropriate setting. Industrial applicants need one year of supervised field training experience. All applicants must have five years of professional experience, four years of which must be postdoctoral. Experience in independent private practice can be counted *only* if it has been preceded by three years (including the internship year) of supervised experience. Applicants must presently be engaged in the specialty in which they were trained and in which they are applying for the diploma, show evidence of continuing education, and be APA members.

There are two major differences between the criteria that take effect in 1980 and prior criteria. First, before 1980, applicants from programs considered primarily psychological in nature but not APA-approved or in psychology departments were considered for the ABPP diploma. Since ABPP has adopted the criteria of the 1977 Education and Credentialing Conference (see Chapter Three), however, applicants who did not graduate from programs clearly labeled as psychology programs may be declared ineligible, despite whatever other licensing or psychological credentials have been obtained since completion of the degree.

Second, according to the new criteria, candidates are required to become a diplomate in the area in which they received graduate training or have authorized approval from a director of a program in which they wish to take the specialty that they have completed the equivalent doctoral-level work; for example, a person trained as a school psychologist applying for the diplomate in counseling psychology would be required to provide a statement from the director of a counseling psychology program that the training of the candidate was equivalent to the training of a counseling psychologist. Under the old requirements, an applicant could apply for an examination in an area other than the one in which he or she was trained.

Persons seeking to be an ABPP diplomate must be able to document the 1,800 hours of required internship health service experience, even if they graduated from a clearly labeled psychology program. Note that more hours are required here than for APA-approved internships in either school or counseling psychology (see Chapter Seven). Careful documentation of supervised professional experience following the receipt of the degree is also necessary. A prospective candidate should have a clearly documented psychologist as a supervisor; otherwise, at some later time, the candidate may have to argue with the ABPP over whether a psychologist was actually supervising the candidate.

Candidates who believe that they qualify for the examination should submit an initial application with a fee of $150. If the applicant is determined to meet the qualification standards, a work sample is requested. "To provide substantive content for the examination, the candidate must present one or more work samples of his or her typical practice as a professional psychologist. The samples usually will consist of a verbatim or summarized report of interactions and may be accompanied by audio tape, video tape, motion picture, or other indepth depiction of the candidate's activity" (American Board of Professional Psychology, 1978). The work sample must be accompanied by an additional fee of $150.

After the work sample is submitted, an examining committee of at least three diplomates will be appointed. This committee will include one experienced examiner designated as chair and two other examiners whose orientation and approach in professional practice are similar to the candidate's. The examining committee may request more extensive work samples if they feel more information is needed to evaluate the candidate's competence.

Arrangements must be made with the ABPP as to the location of the examination. In cases where appropriate local examiners cannot be found, the candidate must bear the costs of traveling to another examination site or help defray the travel costs of examiners who come to his or her location. The examination covers three major areas: the effectiveness of the candidate's intervention based on a realistic assessment of the problem presented, awareness of the relevance of psychological research and theory, and sensitivity to the ethical implications of professional practice. To assess the first area, a field examination, in addition to the submitted work sample, is usually required in which the candidate demonstrates how he or she performs professionally. Interventions such as assessment, counseling, psychotherapy, and organizational consultation have all been used for field assessments.

The last two areas are assessed in ways similar to traditional graduate school oral examinations. A broad range of questions in the areas of research, theory, ethics, and professional practice are asked, especially questions that have the candidate apply these areas to his or her specialty. Candidates who do not pass the examination may request reexamination, in which case a new examination fee of $150 is charged and a new examining committee appointed.

The diplomate may be revoked when the recipient is no longer judged to meet the standard of practice on which the diplomate was based. Full details on application procedures and policies of the board may be obtained by writing to the American Board of Professional Psychology, 2025 I Street, N.W., Suite 405, Washington, D.C. 20006.

The diplomate has at least three major benefits. First, more than any other form of credentialing, it represents excellence in the field of psychology and is so recognized by being awarded annually at a special ceremony at the APA convention. Second, as noted in Chapter Three, a diplomate qualifies for licensing without examination in most states. Third, in a number of state civil service and other positions, a diplomate automatically receives a higher professional classification and thus has a competitive advantage over other applicants. A diplomate also receives a higher salary or higher fees for services rendered in these positions.

In its more than thirty years of existence, the ABPP has certainly had a fair share of complaints regarding its criteria and examinations, especially the latter, and the board has tried to be responsive. By stipulating that the examining committee include persons whose orientation and approach in professional practice are similar to the candidate's, the board tried to address complaints that the examinations focused on the examiners' competencies rather than the examinee's. For example, a community-oriented psychologist might be examined by a psychoanalytically oriented committee and, not surprisingly, be judged to perform poorly. In some cases, counseling psychology candidates were examined by a committee composed totally of clinical psychologists. Even now, candidates who engage in few, if any, traditional psychological services rarely have committees that are truly representative of their specialized practices. Recent ABPP examinees generally agree that the approval process is greatly facilitated by submitting a work sample and engaging in a field assessment that includes some relatively traditional work in assessment, psychotherapy, or consultation.

Many of the other complaints and criticisms have pertained to an individual examinee's qualifications, work sample, or examination performance. Until the examination of competence in professional psychology has broader approval, the ABPP procedures will doubtlessly continue to be criticized by both successful and unsuccessful candidates.

National Register for Health Service Providers in Psychology

A national register of health-service-providing psychologists was proposed in the early 1970s to deal with the concerns of legislators and medical colleagues who felt that many psychologists were not at all trained in providing mental health services. These concerns were heightened after the late 1960s, when psychologists were directly reimbursed for providing health services with increasing frequency and were being considered in proposed national health insurance plans. It was argued that psychologists who were legitimate health service providers must be identified in some way, and that only with self-policing could convincing arguments be made to insurers and medical personnel that some psychologists should be reimbursed for mental health services. These issues have become more prominent as more and more professionals compete for fewer mental health dollars (Levin, 1979).

The major function of the register, then, has been to designate licensed and certified psychologists as health service providers. This information is provided to the public, including national organizations, state legislators, and insurance companies. However, "the list is not nor does it claim to be inclusive of all psychologists who meet the criteria. It is not designed nor does it purport in any way to evaluate the quality or competence of the services provided by anyone listed or not listed in the register. It is not intended as an employment register" (Council for the National Register of Health Service Providers in Psychology, 1978, p. vii).

When the register was established in 1975, any person already licensed or certified as a psychologist in a state could apply if he or she had 3,000 hours of supervised experience in a health service setting. During the first three years (1975-1977) of the register, persons without a doctoral degree were considered if they (1) had at least six years' experience in the field, (2) had earned the advanced degree before January 1, 1969, and (3) had been certified or licensed as of January 1, 1975.

As of January 1, 1978, the criteria for listing in the register became more stringent. Listing in the register now requires that the practitioner (1) be currently licensed by a state psychology licensing board for independent practice; (2) hold a doctoral degree in psychology from a regionally accredited educational institution; and (3) have two years of supervised experience in health service, of which at least one year is postdoctoral and at least one year (either pre- or postdoctoral) is in an organized health service training program. An internship or its equivalent must have included 1,500 hours of training that were completed in no more than two consecutive years in an organized health service setting. Supervised experience, whether pre- or postdoctoral, must have involved direct, formal contact with a senior psychologist responsible for the development of the supervisee. Only supervision of direct professional service is acceptable; classroom or practicum experience or other course-related experiences are *not* acceptable, nor is personal growth experience, such as personal therapy or encounter groups. The supervisors must be licensed or certified and meet the qualifications for practice in their respective professions. Those listed in the National Register qualify as supervisors.

The fee for registration as of January 1, 1980, is a total of $135—$60 to accompany the application for the credential review and $75 if approved. An annual renewal fee of $15 is charged for maintaining an up-to-date listing. The application process requires the candidate to provide information regarding the psychology internship, other supervised health service experience, professional experience, and degree and licensing status. Confirmation-of-supervision forms must be completed by the applicant's intern supervisors and other supervisors of postdoctoral experience.

The major advantage of listing in the register is qualification for reimbursement by several major reimbursers of health services, such as the Civilian Health and Medical Program of the Uniformed Services, Aetna, and Blue Cross/Blue Shield, in those states where psychologists are directly reimbursed (in some states psychologists are indirectly reimbursed through a supervisory psychiatrist or physician). As of 1979, the APA Committee on Ethics accepts the inclusion on one's professional public statements of the phrase "Listed in the National Register of

Health Service Providers in Psychology." It is presently assumed that if some form of national health insurance is passed that permits psychologists to be reimbursed directly for providing health services, listing in the register may be the primary indication of being a qualified health service provider.

As with licensing and receiving the diploma from the ABPP, the source of the degree has been the major problem encountered by many licensed psychologists applying to the register. As noted in Chapter Three, the register, in its first years of operation, received applications from licensed psychologists presenting thirty-five different academic degrees from thirty-five different majors. This tremendous variability in the credentials of applicants led to the guidelines regarding the designation of psychology programs developed by the 1976 and 1977 Education and Credentialing Conferences. The implementation of the guidelines by the register in 1978 greatly magnified the problem for many licensed persons who did not register before that date or for future licensees who were graduating from programs that were not in full accord with the guidelines.

In the coming years several thousand persons who become licensed or certified as psychologists will undoubtedly be declared ineligible for the National Register of Health Services Providers because they trained in programs not labeled as psychology programs. At least one group of licensed psychologists (in Massachusetts) is petitioning the register to provide a grandparent clause that would apply the initial register requirements for eligibility to those persons who were already in graduate training when the new criteria were implemented.

Applicants should carefully arrange to receive and document the required supervised experience, paying attention to the supervisors' qualifications. Only supervisors who are listed in the national register are automatically acceptable. Experience supervised by non-listed psychologists or other professionals such as social workers, psychiatrists, or counselor educators may be deemed unacceptable. Exceptions can be made under the provision that supervisors meet the qualifications for practice in their respective professions, but there is no clear precedent as to what conditions meet these qualifications.

Licensed or certified psychologists interested in being listed in the register and who believe that they meet the training and supervised experience requirements should simply submit an application. A review committee will then examine the application and may request further clarification or documentation of one's professional credentials. No examination is involved, since the register does not evaluate competence but rather lists psychologists having appropriate training and experience for providing health services.

National Academy of Certified Clinical Mental Health Counselors

In early 1979, the American Mental Health Counselors Association (AMHCA), a division of the APGA, established a National Academy of Certified Clinical Mental Health Counselors, which began to accept candidates on July 1 of that year. The academy is independently incorporated and meets the requirements set by the National Commission for Health Certifying Agencies (see Chapter Two). It is viewed as the mechanism whereby the association can monitor and police itself by setting standards and certifying that people meet those standards. Certification will be granted to those who pass a professional counselor's examination, which is the same four-hour examination currently used to license counselors in Virginia. The application requires an extensive personal portfolio ("New Board to Certify," 1979), and an application fee of $50. A candidate fee (examination fee) of $100 and a registration fee of $50 are also charged, for a total cost of $200. Information on the board and applications may be obtained from the National Academy of Certified Clinical Mental Health Counselors (address in appendix).

At this point, this board essentially provides voluntary certification. Of course, it will overlap to some extent the registry being developed by the APGA, but because it examines candidates, it is a more effective indication of competence and shows that the counselors are responsibly moving to monitor and police themselves. While there is little evidence of conflict at this point, the AMHCA and the APGA must work together to avoid redundancy in certification procedures and factionalism over the definition of counseling. The AMHCA is negotiating with health insurance organizations about third-party reimbursements for services provided by certified clinical mental health counselors.

Clinical Membership in the AAMFT

Clinical membership in the AAMFT has been established as a form of certification, unlike membership in the APA. "The AAMFT, founded in 1942, serves as the professional association for the field of marital and family therapy. As a recognized credentialing organization, it ensures qualified clinicians in the practice of marital and family therapy. This credentialing process serves as 'formal certification' in states and provinces which do not yet have licensure or certification laws. . . . This credentialing process is viewed as a 'right to practice' in these nonlicensed states and provinces" (American Association for Marriage and Family Therapy, 1979b). (See Chapter Five for a discussion of licensing of marriage and family counselors and therapists.)

As of July 1, 1978, eligibility for clinical membership requires an earned master's or doctoral degree in marriage and family therapy from an accredited institution or a master's or doctoral degree from an accredited institution in an allied mental health profession. The applicant's official transcript must establish that the latter type of degree is substantially equivalent to that for the course of study described below. After December 31, 1983, applicants who receive their degree from an allied mental health profession will have to demonstrate that their curriculum fully meets the following course of study, rather than merely being substantially equivalent: a minimum of nine semester hours (or equivalent) in human development, nine semester hours in marital and family studies, nine semester hours in marital and family therapy, three semester hours in professional studies, nine semester hours in supervised clinical work, and six semester hours in research methodology.

In addition to the above academic preparation, the applicant for AAMFT clinical membership shall have completed the following: (1) 200 hours of supervision in the practice of marital and family therapy. No more than 100 hours may be accumulated in group supervision. A maximum of 50 individual hours and 50 group hours may be credited while a student is in a master's program prior to graduation. (2) 1500 hours of clinical experience (defined as face-to-face contact) in the practice of marital and family therapy. 500 of these hours may have been accumulated while the candidate was a student in a master's degree program in marital and family therapy, 250 of these 1500 may be accumulated from the practice of individual psychotherapy. A minimum of 50 cases in marital and family therapy shall have been treated. (3) Two calendar years of work experience after the awarding of the master's degree and while receiving ongoing supervision by an AAMFT approved supervisor. (4) Demonstrated readiness for the independent practice of marital and family therapy [American Association for Marriage and Family Therapy, 1979b].

An applicant must also be endorsed by two clinical members of the AAMFT. Student and associate memberships are also available, which do not certify the right to practice. The major advantages of clinical membership are that licensing by states and reimbursement for services, which are provided by CHAMPUS and some other service providers, become more easy to obtain.

Most of the problems encountered by applicants for AAMFT clinical membership involve the interpretation of "substantial equivalent of course work" and the demonstration of acceptable supervised practice. The term "substantially equivalent" has created for the AAMFT all the problems that psychology licensing boards have in interpreting the term "primarily psychological." The clinical experience requirements are so specific that traditionally trained counselors and psychologists, unless they have arranged for special experience and supervision, do not qualify.

Clinical membership in the AAMFT, as well as the types of credentialing described in the next two sections, requires quite specific training and experience at or beyond the master's-degree level. Without this training, one is simply ineligible for such credentialing. However, while the applicant who is ineligible for the National Register or the ABPP diploma must essentially redo the doctoral degree, the ineligible applicant for AAMFT clinical membership can simply complete supplemental academic course work and obtain the needed experience.

Certification from the American Association of Sex Educators, Counselors, and Therapists

The AASECT was founded in 1967 to develop competence standards for sex educators and counselors. It presently has a membership of over 6,000, with nearly 1,000 certified sex educators, 1,000 certified sex therapists, and approximately 60 certified sex counselors. A national register of these certified members is published annually, and a publication, the *Journal of Sex Education and Therapy,* is published semiannually. Each category of certification (educator, therapist, and counselor) has separate requirements, separate application forms, and application fees (with a fee of $50 for each form of certification).

Certification as a sex counselor has the fewest requirements. (Under the grandparent clause, which expired in June 1980, applicants needed only an undergraduate college degree, experience in group or individual counseling within a recognized agency or institutional setting for a minimum of two years, two letters of reference, and participation in a weekend workshop on human sexuality.) When the grandparent clause expired, two requirements were added: a test of knowledge covering sexual functioning and behavior as well as counseling methods and tools, and a written statement of personal impressions and views of sexual normality.

To qualify as a sex therapist, a person must hold a doctorate or master's degree in a field such as counseling or clinical psychology, social work, nursing, or pastoral, marriage, or mental health counseling; be able to present evidence of having had

100 hours of individual supervision from a qualified sex therapist or 150 group supervision hours (or combination thereof); and fulfill the requirements for certification as a sex counselor.

To become a certified sex educator, the primary qualification is experience in teaching sex education. The minimal educational requirement is as follows: an associate's degree plus five years' experience, a bachelor's degree plus three years' experience, a master's degree plus three years' experience, or a doctorate plus two years' experience. The experience must include conducting workshops, attending institutes, teaching courses, lecturing, contributing to the literature, consulting with others, or being responsible for planning and administering programs. The experience should consist of the development of an interdisciplinary curriculum that reflects methodology conducive to the acquisition of knowledge and that deals with attitudes and values regarding human sexuality. Applicants must also meet the sex counselor requirements.

The organization sponsors national and regional institutes and workshops throughout Canada and the United States, as well as basic and advanced full-semester academic courses in sex education, sex counseling, and sex therapy offered through various universities. In addition to the categories of certified membership, there are membership opportunities for sex researchers, graduate students, and undergraduate students whose research or study is related to the field of sex education, counseling, therapy, and research. (Psychologists and counselors with requirements for and/or interests in continuing education should note that most of AASECT's workshops offer continuing education credits in a variety of professional fields.)

To our knowledge, psychologists and counselors have encountered no significant problems in qualifying for these credentials. As with credentialing by the AAMFT, fairly specific training and experience are necessary. While AASECT certification is frequently listed in one's professional announcements and therefore has public relations value, there are no other readily identified professional privileges. However, certified counselors, therapists, and educators do receive requests to offer specialized educational programs and receive referrals for treatment of sexual dysfunction because of their certification.

Certification from the Commission on Rehabilitation Counselor Certification

The Commission on Rehabilitation Counselor Certification has certified individuals in the profession of rehabilitation counseling since 1974. The commission was an outgrowth of the concerns in the early 1970s of two associations: the National Rehabilitation Counseling Association and the American Rehabilitation Counseling Association. In order to establish national minimum standards, these two associations jointly created a commission for certification. Procedures and standards for certification were prepared by an eighteen-person commission, comprised of five appointees from each parent organization plus three appointees from the American Coalition of Citizens with Disabilities and one appointee each from the Council on Rehabilitation Education, the Council of State Administrators of Vocational Rehabilitation, the Association of Rehabilitation Facilities, the Vocational Association of Nonwhite Rehabilitation Workers, and the National Council on Rehabilitation Education.

Eligibility for certification is based on a combination of the quality of formal training and the amount of acceptable employment experience. A student who has been trained in a master's program in rehabilitation counseling that is accredited by the Council on Rehabilitation Education and who has completed the internship required by such an accredited program is eligible for certification as soon as the degree is completed. Persons having a master's or a bachelor's degree in an area unrelated to rehabilitation counseling must have at least five years of acceptable employment experience, at least one of which must have been completed under the supervision of a certified rehabilitation counselor. Acceptable experience is defined as full-time paid employment or its equivalent in a job in which the person counsels special populations and uses some combination of vocational and rehabilitation methods.

Persons who believe themselves eligible may apply to sit for the certification examination. An application process fee of $35 is required, and a $50 examination fee is charged if an applicant is declared eligible. The examination consists of approximately 300 multiple-choice questions drawn from an item pool developed in a two-year period by over 8,000 rehabilitation counselors, educators, and administrators. Questions are primarily practice based and cover most of the topics listed in the curriculum required for accredited rehabilitation counselor training programs (see Chapter Seven). The certification examination is given each spring and fall at various wheel-chair accessible examination sites.

Candidates who pass examinations are certified for a five-year period; however, as of January 1979, certified rehabilitation counselors must recertify by completing at least thirty hours per year of continuing education workshops, seminars, and the like.

Persons who meet the requirements for educational and employment experiences except for supervision by a certified rehabilitation counselor may submit a plan for receiving this supervision and apply for provisional certification. If the supervision is approved by the commission, candidates will be allowed to sit for the certification examination. If candidates pass the examination, they will receive provisional certificates that will be voided when the supervision plan is completed or after twenty-four months, whichever comes first. In the former case, full certification will be granted; in the latter, all certification will be denied.

Details of the procedures and regulations for certification are found in the mimeographed material "Some Commonly Asked Questions About Rehabilitation Counselor Certification," available from the commission (address in appendix).

Because this certification is fairly new, few problems for applicants have been identified. Although specialized training and experience are required, they can be gained in a relatively short period—one to two years, depending on one's past education and experience. Although this certification does not have any professional advantages beyond those of status and public information, its requirements will probably be similar, if not identical, to requirements proposed for licensure as rehabilitation counselors. The existence of this type of certification can probably play a major role in convincing legislators of the adequacy of the profession's self-policing efforts and may facilitate legislators' willingness to support licensure for rehabilitation counselors.

9

Prospects for Licensing and Certification in the 1980s

As we enter the 1980s, three major credentialing issues are facing psychologists and counselors: sunset legislation, health insurance payments, and consumerism.

Most immediately, as described in Chapter Three, licensing boards will be increasingly scrutinized as a result of sunset legislation. Psychology is confronted with the issue now; counseling, in contrast, must anticipate sunset even before counselors are licensed in most states. As demonstrated in South Dakota, Florida, Kansas, and Alaska, state legislatures will be more than willing to allow licensure laws to lapse unless the profession can agree on qualification and assessment procedures. Accordingly, these matters must be resolved before a sunset hearing takes place so that the best possible case can be made for the profession with the broadest support from its practitioners. As described in Chapter Six, all segments of the profession must be consulted and included in the sunset preparation. However, difficult choices must be made concerning the kinds of data to gather and the kinds of collaboration to pursue.

The professions of counseling and psychology can benefit from learning about each other's experiences in coping with challenges to their licensure activities. Must both the American Psychological Association (APA) and the American Personnel and Guidance Association (APGA) separately, and probably redundantly, develop materials and aids for assisting states and local organizations in their credentialing difficulties?

The second major issue confronting psychologists and counselors concerns health insurance and third-party payments. Will there soon be a national health insurance plan? Will mental health be covered? If so, whose services will be covered? The current status of national health insurance is indefinite, with strong, knowledgeable views ranging from the inevitability of national health insurance to its impossibility.

More people agree that some form of national health insurance will be passed by Congress in the 1980s, although it may not be comprehensive. Whether out-patient mental health services will be covered (and if so, by whom) is certainly not clear. As Hogan (1979a) notes, the possibility that mental health services will be included is stimulating a marked amount of strife among the mental health professions. Bread-and-butter issues are clearly involved. If one profession can exclude others, it can establish a more monopolistic position. Psychiatry, psychology, mental health counseling, social work, and psychiatric nursing will no doubt all be involved. The biggest loser from this strife would be the public, which may find that mental health services are excluded from national health insurance because the Congress found that the easiest way to avoid fighting among the mental health professions was to exclude any coverage of their services! Such a possibility is not unlikely, since mental health services are *not* the major reason that most taxpayers support national health insurance.

Equally important is the fact that the licensing of mental

health professions is inextricably related to national health insurance, since reimbursement by third-party payers, that is, insurance companies, has usually been linked to the licensing of the profession.

Any exclusions of professions from national health insurance coverage could also change traditional hiring patterns radically. For example, why would a mental health center continue to hire counseling psychologists if national health insurance reimburses only the services rendered by clinical psychologists or psychiatrists? Why would a university counseling center continue to hire counselors if their work is not reimbursable when that of psychologists or psychiatrists is?

The third issue faced by psychologists and counselors is the consumer movement. Does credentialing make a significant difference to the recipients of mental health or counseling services? The consumer often feels that he or she is protected only by rhetoric, which ultimately seems to be a profession's attempt to minimize competition and enhance its own financial base. Worse yet, while licensing acts may exclude professionals who might be competent to provide services, persons who may have appropriate training and education but are nonetheless incompetent might be licensed. The lack of effective mechanisms for assessing competence may leave the consumer unconvinced that the present forms of credentialing are in his or her best interests.

Some attempts have been made to address the issue of competence evaluation. For example, in early 1980 the APA established a Task Force on Competency Assessment. Just as important as assessment systems are effective monitoring or peer review systems. Currently psychology has two developing models for peer review. The Civilian Health and Medical Program of the Uniformed Services (CHAMPUS) model, although meant only for persons with CHAMPUS insurance coverage, is a highly articulated set of guidelines for appropriate practice. Although consumers did not help develop those guidelines, they could make valuable contributions to such efforts. State professional standards review committees (PSRCs) also provide a model for consumers, insurance companies, and other interested parties for developing policies and procedures for increasing the responsiveness of professions to consumers' concerns.

There are two problems with the CHAMPUS and PSRC models. First, they are not routine checks on professionals' practice; they are only used when there appears to be a problem. Presumably many problems exist that are not called to the attention of these peer review organizations. A peer review system must operate routinely, not only in answer to a grievance. Second, effective peer review procedures need to evaluate actual professional behavior (safeguarding, of course, consumer confidentiality), not just written documents, as they generally do now. There may not be (and undoubtedly is not) a close correspondence between what a psychologist, counselor, or psychiatrist writes on a treatment summary sheet and what that person actually does in treatment. Peer review must do more than simply shape written behavior.

Quarrels between professions also pose problems. Certainly the recent case brought by psychologists against Blue Cross and Blue Shield in Virginia publicized psychiatrists' charges about the inability of psychologists to provide mental health services. Weigel (1977) also cited some of the acerbic exchanges between psychologists and counselors. Rather than each profession's unique contributions to mental health services, what seems to get aired in public is each profession's belief that it is the only suitable profession for providing psychotherapeutic or counseling services. If licensing, national health insurance, and consumerism issues are responded to in terms of narrow interest groups, or even by, for example, alliances of psychiatrists and psychologists against counselors and social workers, the greatest loser will be the public. Consumers may lose both legislative protection and health insurance coverage of mental health services as lawmakers seek to avoid professional infighting.

We have been greatly concerned that psychology has treated counseling as it was treated by psychiatry. There has been too little recognition that some well-trained, competent persons in both professions have common concerns for the well-being of their clienteles. At present, psychology is probably more politically powerful than counseling, more mature in licensure issues, and more successful in gaining public attention. If psychology, from its position of strength, continues to exclude appropriately trained and competent counseling colleagues, it then reflects medicine's views toward psychology, which psychology itself has found invalid and inappropriate.

At the same time, counselor training programs must decide whether they are training counselors or psychologists. Until now, many counselor training programs have had it both ways, promoting themselves as centers for training counselors but becoming very concerned when their graduates are not allowed to sit for psychology certification exams. Counselor training programs that wish to train psychologists need to employ psychologically trained and oriented faculty and to follow the spirit, as well as the letter, of the criteria set forth in the "blue book" (Wellner, 1978). We strongly feel that, while the concerns of counseling and psychology may overlap, the public will benefit if each profession remains separate with clearly identified training models and competencies. Consumers will be greatly assisted if each profession clearly identifies and enhances its unique contributions rather than offering only the training in traditional psychotherapy now provided by many different kinds of mental health professionals.

A current dilemma for all mental health professions is the sparse investigation of whether different professions actually make unique contributions to mental health services. With no consensus among the professions on the qualifications required for mental health services, and with no acceptable competency-based examination (Hogan, 1979b), arguments about which professions should have what professional privileges tend to be self-serving rhetoric rather than the data-based analyses one might expect from supposedly scientifically based professions. Given the present paucity of such data, it is unlikely that we will soon have empirical evidence to determine (1) who should be licensed, (2) who should be included in national health insurance, and (3) who can provide the most effective and reasonable services for consumers.

Throughout this book we have addressed the need for

collaboration and mutual respect among the different mental health professions. At present there are many expensive and somewhat redundant efforts, such as the development of the certification examination by the American Mental Health Counselors Association and the development of a more valid psychology examination by the Professional Examination Service. Just as the Council on Postsecondary Accreditation is working to increase the collaboration among the groups that accredit university training programs, more collaborative efforts are needed to determine appropriate training and to review examination and monitoring systems for all mental health professions.

Although we now lack the data for more competency-based assessments, we must not give up our efforts to obtain such data. Regrettably, the professions of counseling and psychology have seldom, if ever, reacted to sunset, national health insurance, and consumer issues by collecting appropriate data.

Many questions can be answered even with our present rudimentary measurement techniques; data from our principal investigations would allow us to judge far more wisely the training and skills that psychologists and counselors should have for providing services. Can consumers make satisfactory and effective judgments if they are provided with extensive information about the services that they are to receive? Are consumers more satisfied or helped by the services of licensed or unlicensed persons? How many competent service providers would a competency-based evaluation identify? What is the relationship between professional education and properly assessed professional competence? What counseling and psychological services are not now being offered by credentialed personnel? Are innovations in training and services less evident in accredited programs and among licensed practitioners?

Unless psychology and counseling collaborate, and unless we answer these questions and act according to the data we collect, the future of credentialing and licensing in psychology and counseling will at best be a continuation of the present deficiencies and at worst a loss to both consumers and the professions of the benefits of fair, objective legislative and public recognition.

Appendix: Agency and Organization Addresses

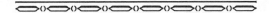

Advisory Committee on Accreditation and Institutional Eligibility
Division of Eligibility and Agency Evaluation
U.S. Office of Education
Bureau of Higher and Continuing Education
Washington, D.C. 20202

American Association of Marriage and Family Therapists
Upland, Calif. 91786

American Association of Sex Educators, Counselors, and Therapists
5010 Wisconsin Ave., N.W., Suite 304
Washington, D.C. 20016

Note: Licensing boards are maintained in each state for all licensed professions. A master list of psychology licensing boards may be obtained from the Professional Affairs Office of the American Psychological Association.

American Board of Professional Psychology
2025 I St., N.W., Suite 405
Washington, D.C. 20006

American Council on Education
One Dupont Circle, N.W.
Washington, D.C. 20036

American Personnel and Guidance Association
Two Skyline Place, Suite 400
5203 Leesburg Pike
Falls Church, Va. 22041

American Psychological Association
1200 17th St., N.W.
Washington, D.C. 20036

Council of Graduate Schools in the U.S.
One Dupont Circle, N.W.
Washington, D.C. 20036

Council of Postsecondary Accreditation
One Dupont Circle, N.W.
Washington, D.C. 20036

Council of State Governments
Headquarters Office
Iron Works
Lexington, Ky. 40578

Council on Rehabilitation Education
                    and
Commission on Rehabilitation Counselor Certification
8 South Michigan Ave., Suite 3301
Chicago, Ill. 60603

National Academy of Certified Clinical Mental Health
    Counselors
10700 62nd St.
Temple Terrace, Fla. 33617

Professional Examination Service
475 Riverside Dr.
New York, N.Y. 10027

References

"ACES Guidelines for Doctoral Preparation in Counselor Education." *Counselor Education and Supervision,* 1978, *17,* 163-165.

"ACES Pilot Study Begins." *APGA Guidepost,* April 26, 1979, p. 3.

Albee, G. W. "The Uncertain Future of the MA Clinical Psychologist." *Professional Psychology,* 1977, *8,* 122-124.

American Association for Marriage and Family Therapy. *Marital and Family Therapy: State Licensing and Certification Model Legislation.* Upland, Calif.: American Association for Marriage and Family Therapy, 1979a.

American Association for Marriage and Family Therapy. *Membership Standards Brochure.* Upland, Calif.: American Association for Marriage and Family Therapy, 1979b.

American Board of Professional Psychology. *Policies and Procedures for the Creation of Diplomates in Professional Psychology.* Washington, D.C.: American Board of Professional Psychology, 1978.

American Council on Education. *Accredited Institutions of Postsecondary Education.* Washington, D.C.: American Council on Education, 1979.

American Psychological Association. "Joint Report of the APA and CSPA Committee on Legislation." *American Psychologist,* 1955, *10,* 727-756.

American Psychological Association. *Ethical Standards of Psychologists.* Washington, D.C.: American Psychological Association, 1977a.

American Psychological Association. *Standards for Providers of Psychological Services.* Washington, D.C.: American Psychological Association, 1977b.

American Psychological Association. "Resolution on the Master's Level Issue. Council of Representatives." January 28-30, 1977c.

American Psychological Association. *Report of the Committee on State Legislation.* Washington, D.C.: American Psychological Association, 1978.

American Psychological Association. *Criteria for Accreditation of Doctoral Training Programs and Internships in Professional Psychology.* Washington, D.C.: American Psychological Association, 1979.

American Psychological Association, Committee on State Legislation. *Sunset: Complete Report.* Washington, D.C.: American Psychological Association, 1979.

American Psychological Association, Council of Representatives. "Policy on Training for Psychologists Wishing to Change Their Specialty." January 23-25, 1976.

American Psychological Association, Division of Counseling Psychology. "Licensing and Certification of Psychologists—A Position Statement." *Counseling Psychologist,* 1975, *5* (3), 135.

American Psychological Association, Division of Counseling Psychology. "The Defining Characteristics of Counseling Psychologists." Washington, D.C.: American Psychological Association, 1977.

American Psychological Association, Office of Educational Affairs. *Sourcebook on the Master's Level Issue.* Washington, D.C.: American Psychological Association, 1977.

"AMHCA Seeks Amendment to Health Bill." *APGA Guidepost,* January 17, 1980, pp. 1, 16.

"APGA Board Reconsiders ACES Role." *APGA Guidepost,* April 26, 1979, pp. 1, 15.

"APGA Registry Committee Meets." *APGA Guidepost,* March 1, 1979, p. 1.

Arbuckle, D. S. "Counselor Licensure: To Be or Not to Be." *Personnel and Guidance Journal,* 1977, *55,* 581-585.

"Arkansas to License Counselors." *APGA Guidepost,* June 14, 1979, pp. 1, 7.

Asher, J. K. "The Coming Exclusion of Counselors from the Mental Health Care System." *American Mental Health Counselors Association Journal,* 1979, *1,* 53-60.

Autor, S., and Zide, E. "Master's Level Professional Training in Clinical Psychology and Community Mental Health." *Professional Psychology,* 1974, *5,* 115-121.

Bartlett, C. J. "I'm Mad as Hell and I'm Not Going to Take It Anymore." *Industrial Organizational Psychologist,* 1979, *16,* 26-28.

Blum, D. "Clearwater Okays Tougher Psychology Standards." *St. Petersburg Times,* July 20, 1979, p. B-1.

Brown, R. A., and Briley, P. L. "Continuing Education Activities for Maryland Psychologists: A Survey." *Professional Psychology,* 1979, *10,* 285-292.

Bullington, J. "The Future of the Master's Degree in Psychology: A Review from the Outside." *American Psychologist,* 1979, *34,* 270.

Carlson, H. S. "The AASPB Story." *American Psychologist,* 1978, *33,* 486-495.

Carroll, M. R., Halligan, F. G., and Griggs, S. A. "The Licensure Issue: How Real Is It?" *Personnel and Guidance Journal,* 1977, *55,* 577-580.

Carsten, A. "A Public Perspective on Scoring the Licensing Exam." *Professional Psychology,* 1978, *9,* 531-532.

Cattell, J. M. "Retrospect: Psychology as a Profession." *Journal of Consulting Psychology,* 1937, *1,* 1-3.

Claiborn, W., and Stricker, G. "Professional Standards Review Organizations, Peer Review, and CHAMPUS." *Professional Psychology,* 1979, *10,* 631-639.

Cleveland, S. E. "Article Under Attack." *APGA Guidepost,* February 15, 1979, p. 2.

Cohen, H. S. *A Proposal for Credentialing Health Manpower.* Washington, D.C.: U.S. Department of Health, Education, and Welfare, 1976.

Commission on Human Resources. *Doctorate Records File.* Washington, D.C.: National Academy of Sciences, 1975.

Commission on Standards and Accreditation, Association for Counselor Education and Supervision. "Standards for the Preparation of Counselors and Other Personnel Services Specialists." *Personnel and Guidance Journal,* 1977, *55,* 596-601.

"Cooperation to Be Theme of Conference." *Accreditation* [Newsletter of the Council on Postsecondary Accreditation], Winter 1978, p. 7.

Cottingham, H. F., and Warner, R. W. "APGA and Counselor Licensure: A Status Report." *Personnel and Guidance Journal,* 1978, *56,* 604-607.

Council for the National Register of Health Service Providers in Psychology. *National Register of Health Service Providers in Psychology.* Washington, D.C.: National Register of Health Service Providers in Psychology, 1978.

Council on Rehabilitation Education, Inc. *Accreditation Manual for Rehabilitation Counselor Education Programs.* Chicago: Council of Rehabilitation Education, Inc., 1978.

"Council Votes to Scrub Work on State Licensing Standards, Approve Two Divisions." *APA Monitor,* November 1979, pp. 1, 7.

"Counselors to Join Social Workers." *APGA Guidepost,* October 11, 1979, pp. 1, 4.

Cummings, N. "The Undoing of Clinical Psychology." *APA Monitor,* December 1979, p. 2.

"Demographic Study Shows APGA Status." *APGA Guidepost,* October 25, 1979, p. 5.

Dörken, H. "Avenues to Legislative Success." *American Psychologist,* 1977, *32,* 738-745.

Dörken, H. "Why the Sun Didn't Set in the West." *The Clinical Psychologist,* 1979, *31,* 774-784.

Dörken, H., and Morrison, D. "JCAH Standards for Accreditation of Psychiatric Facilities." *American Psychologist,* 1976, *31,* 774-784.

Ehrenreich, B., and English, D. *Witches, Midwives, and Nurses: A History of Women Healers.* Old Westbury, N.Y.: Feminist Press, 1973.

Farmer, A. "A Profession Still in Diapers." *APA Monitor,* November 1979, p. 12.

Fiester, A. R. "JCAH Standards for Accreditation of Community Mental Health Service Programs." *American Psychologist,* 1978, *33,* 1114-1121.

Flexner, A. *Medical Education in the United States and Canada.* New York: Carnegie Foundation, 1910.

Foltz, D. "Sun Sets on Psychology Licensing Boards in South Dakota and Florida." *APA Monitor,* September/October 1979, pp. 14, 31.

Forster, J. R. "Counselor Credentialing Revisited." *Personnel and Guidance Journal,* 1978, *56,* 593-598.

Gazda, G. M. "Licensure/Certification for Counseling Psychologists and Counselors." *Personnel and Guidance Journal,* 1977, *55,* 570.

Gies, W. *Dental Education in the United States and Canada.* New York: Carnegie Foundation, 1926.

Gross, S. J. "Professional Disclosure: An Alternative to Licensing." *Personnel and Guidance Journal,* 1977, *55,* 586-588.

Gross, S. J. "The Myth of Professional Licensing." *American Psychologist,* 1978, *33,* 1009-1016.

"Guidelines for Doctoral Preparation in Counselor Education." *Counselor Education and Supervision,* 1978, *17,* 163-168.

Hays, J. R., and Schreiner, D. "Comparison of Degrees Received and Performance on Licensing Examination." *Psychological Reports,* 1977, *40,* 42.

Hogan, D. B. "Licensing Mental Therapists." *New York Times,* July 18, 1979a, p. A-23.

Hogan, D. B. *The Regulation of Psychotherapies: A Handbook of State Licensure Laws.* 4 vols. Cambridge, Mass.: Ballinger, 1979b.

Hollis, J. W., and Wantz, R. A. *Counselor Education Directory,*

1977: Personnel and Programs. (3rd ed.) Muncie, Ind.: Accelerated Development, 1977.

Illich, I. *Medical Nemesis.* New York: Random House, 1976.

Ivey, A. "Credentialism and the Effective Delivery of Human Services." Draft of policy paper for National Institute of Human Services, 1978.

Koocher, G. "Credentialing in Psychology: Close Encounters with Competence?" *American Psychologist,* 1979, *34,* 696-702.

Korman, M. (Ed.). *Levels and Patterns of Professional Training in Psychology.* Washington, D.C.: American Psychological Association, 1973.

Krause, E. A. *Power and Illness: The Political Sociology of Health and Medical Care.* New York: Elsevier, 1977.

Krueger, A. H. "Letters and Comments." *Personnel and Guidance Journal,* 1967, *45,* 1033-1044.

Lahman, F. G. *Licensure Requirements for Psychologists: USA and Canada.* Evansville, Ind.: University of Evansville Press, 1978.

Levin, H. "War Between the Shrinks." *New York,* May 21, 1979, pp. 52-54.

"Licensing Bill Goes to Senate." *APGA Guidepost,* June 14, 1979, pp. 1, 4.

Licensure Committee Action Packet. Washington, D.C.: American Personnel and Guidance Association, 1979.

Lorion, R. "Community Psychology's Maturation as a Discipline and Profession." *APA Division of Community Psychology Newsletter,* 1979, *12* (3), 3-5.

Mackin, P. K. "Occupational Licensing: A Warning." *Personnel and Guidance Journal,* 1976, *54,* 507-511.

McTeer, W. "A Survey of Graduate School Opinion Regarding Professional Training Below the Doctorate Level." *American Psychologist,* 1952, *7,* 14-19.

Matarazzo, J. D. "Higher Education, Professional Accreditation, and Licensure." *American Psychologist,* 1977, *32,* 856-859.

Moore, B. V. "The Master's Degree in Psychology." *American Psychologist,* 1954, *9,* 120-122.

Moore, P. "Snapshot Dan Hogan." *APA Monitor,* September/ October 1979, pp. 15, 36-37, 44.

"National Written Examination." *American Association of State Psychology Boards Newsletter,* 1978, *14* (1), 9-15.

"New Board to Certify." *APGA Guidepost,* March 1, 1979, p. 1.

"New Hampshire Rehabilitation Counselors Gain Licensure." *APGA Guidepost,* October 25, 1979, pp. 1, 9.

O'Keefe, A. M., and McCullough, S. J. "Physician Domination in the Health Care Industry: The Pursuit of Antitrust Redress." *Professional Psychology,* 1979, *10,* 605-618.

Patterson, C. H. "Distinctions and Commonalities Between Counseling and Psychotherapy." In G. G. Garwell, N. R. Gramsky, and P. Mathieu-Coughlin (Eds.), *The Counselor's Handbook.* New York: Intext, 1974.

"Pre-legislative Summary Spotlighted at Meeting." *APGA Guidepost,* February 15, 1979, pp. xx-1.

"Professional Examination Service Issues and Activities." *American Association of State Psychology Boards Newsletter,* 1978, *13* (2), 10-13.

Randolph, D. L. "The Sleeping Giant Awakens." *APA Division of Community Psychology Newsletter,* 1979, *12* (3), 14-15.

Reed, A. Z. *Training for the Public Profession of the Law.* New York: Carnegie Foundation, 1921.

"Rehabilitation Programs Now Accredited." *APGA Guidepost,* October 11, 1979, p. 2.

"Requirements for Licensing Psychologists Are Ruled Invalid." *St. Louis Post-Dispatch,* April 16, 1979, p. 11.

Rogers, C. R. "Some New Challenges." *American Psychologist,* 1973, *28,* 379-387.

Scelsa, J. V. "Saga of a Shingle." *APGA Guidepost,* September 27, 1979, p. 2.

Shimberg, B., and Roederer, D. *Occupational Licensing: Questions a Legislature Should Ask.* Lexington, Ky.: Council of State Governments, 1978.

Smith, R. C. "Psychology and the Courts." *Professional Psychology,* 1978, *9,* 489-497.

Sourcebook, Education and Credentialing in Psychology. Washington, D.C.: American Psychological Association, 1976.

Sourcebook II, Education and Credentialing in Psychology. Washington, D.C.: American Psychological Association, 1977.

"Standards for Preparation of Counselors and Other Personnel Services Specialists." *Personnel and Guidance Journal,* 1977, *55* (10), 597-601.

Stripling, R. O. "Standards and Accreditation in Counselor Education: A Proposal." *Personnel and Guidance Journal,* 1978, *56,* 608-611.

"Sunset Thunder." *Professionally Speaking* [Newsletter of Office of Professional Affairs, American Psychological Association], August 1979, p. 1.

Swanson, D. C. "A Case Supporting Licensure." *APGA Guidepost,* August 19, 1976, p. 5.

Sweeney, T. J., and Sturdevant, A. D. "Licensure in the Helping Professions: Anatomy of an Issue." *Personnel and Guidance Journal,* 1974, *52,* 575-580.

Sweeney, T. J., and Witmer, J. M. "Who Says You're a Counselor?" *Personnel and Guidance Journal,* 1977, *55,* 589-591, 594.

Tabachnik, L. "Licensing in the Legal and Medical Professions, 1820-1860: A Historical Case Study." In J. Gerstle and G. Jacobs (Eds.), *Professions for the People.* Cambridge, Mass.: Schenkman, 1976.

Terris, L. D. "The National Licensing Examination." *Professional Psychology,* 1973, *4,* 386-391.

Thompson, A. A., and Super, D. E. (Eds.). *The Professional Preparation of Counseling Psychologists* (Grayston Conference). New York: Bureau of Publications, Teachers College, Columbia University, 1964.

"Unit to Study Licensing." *APGA Guidepost,* April 13, 1978, p. 8.

Van Hoose, W. H., and Kottler, J. A. *Ethical and Legal Issues in Counseling and Psychotherapy.* San Francisco: Jossey-Bass, 1977.

Warnath, C. F. "Licensing: Learning the Game of Politics and Compromise." *Personnel and Guidance Journal,* 1978, *57,* 50-53.

Weigel, R. G. "I Have Seen the Enemy and They Is Us—and Everyone Else." *Counseling Psychologist,* 1977, *7* (2), 50-52.

Wellner, A. M. (Ed.). *Education and Credentialing in Psychology: Preliminary Report of a Meeting.* Washington, D.C.: Office of Professional Affairs, American Psychological Association, 1976.

Wellner, A. M. (Ed.). *Education and Credentialing in Psychology II: Report of a Meeting.* Washington, D.C.: Office of Professional Affairs, American Psychological Association, 1977.

Wellner, A. M. (Ed.). *Education and Credentialing in Psychology: Proposal for a National Commission in Education and Credentialing in Psychology.* Washington, D.C.: American Psychological Association, 1978.

Wiens, A. N. "Toward a Definition of Training in Professional Psychology." Portland, Oreg.: American Association of State Psychology Boards, January 1977. Mimeograph.

Witmer, J. M. "Power, Love, Money and Politics." *APGA Licensure Action Line,* 1978-1979, No's. 1-4.

Woods, P. J. "A History of APA's Concern with the Master's Degree: Or, 'Discharged with Thanks.' " *American Psychologist,* 1971, *26,* 696-707.

Index